Personnel Systems and Records
Third edition

Personnel Systems and Records

Compiled by The Industrial Society
Third edition by Barbara Dyer

Gower Press

First published 1969 by Gower Press Ltd
as *Design of Personnel Systems and Records*
Second edition 1973
Third edition 1979

British Library Cataloguing in Publication Data

Industrial Society
   Personnel systems and records.—3rd ed.
   1. Personnel records—Great Britain
   I. Title II. Dyer, Barbara III. Design of
   personnel systems and records
   651.5   HF5549.5.P4

ISBN 0 566 02106 4

Filmset by Inforum Ltd, Portsmouth
Printed in Great Britain by
Biddles Ltd, Guildford, Surrey

Contents

Illustrations

Foreword

By John Garnett, Director, The Industrial Society

Record keeping is not the primary function of the personnel department. Personnel management today must be concerned with the total effectiveness of the work force in achieving its company's objectives of the creation of wealth. However, in order to achieve this task, there is a need for basic records of the people involved in the enterprise. These records should contain only that information which can aid decision taking, and this is the primary role of the records, which need to be kept as simple as possible.

This book sets out the experience of the 15,000 member companies of The Industrial Society. It has now been up-dated and will serve, as it has in the past, as a vital guide to all who are responsible for the personnel side of their company.

The subsidiary role of the personnel records is to fulfil the requirements of Government departments such as the Inland Revenue, the Department of Health and Social Security and HM Factories Inspectorate. By keeping records in a simple and ingenious manner, time will be saved and paper work reduced, and there will be less clerical work load. This will allow those of us who are personnel officers and managers to spend less time sitting in offices and handling paper, and will allow more time for us to be down in the factory and the offices where people actually work.

Acknowledgements

Grateful acknowledgements are due to the following organisations for their assistance and co-operation in providing material for publication in this book:

Anson Systems Division, OCE Skycopy BV
The 600 Group Limited
Greater London Council
Inbucon Limited
Marconi Company Limited
Richard Costain Limited
Twinlock Group
Williams Lea Group

The forms shown in Figures 1:1, 3:3, 3:4, 3:7, 5:8, 5:9, 5:10, 8:4, 8:5, 8:6, 8:7, 8:11 and 8:12 are Crown copyright and are reproduced with the permission of the Controller of Her Majesty's Stationery Office. Thanks are also due to the British Institute of Management, Royal Society for the Prevention of Accidents, and to Kalamazoo Limited, The Copeland-Chatterson Co. Ltd., C.W. Cave & Co. Ltd., Kardex Systems (UK) Limited and Moore Paragon UK Limited, suppliers of business forms and record systems, for providing examples for illustrations.

Publisher's Note

The illustrative material in this book is drawn from actual documents used by companies, to whom acknowledgements are expressed on the previous page, and forms required to be completed by statute and available from the respective government departments.

The need for a standard format in book reproduction means that the size and proportion of many documents have had to be modified. The essential information carried by each form, however, remains unaltered. Firms using this book to design or adapt their own systems and records will, of course, draw up forms of a shape and size to suit their own requirements, adding appropriate data covering company name, reference numbers or dates, specific instructions, etc.

In describing specific government forms and records it has been necessary to refer to the statutory obligations on employers for completing and keeping these records. It should be stressed, however, that these references to the law are not comprehensive, nor were they meant to be.

The law applies differently to different types of firms and industries in various circumstances and there are exceptions. Detailed information may be obtained from publications available free of charge from the relevant government offices. Leaflets concerning the Employment Protection Act, Trade Union and Labour Relations Act and the Employment Protection (Consolidation) Act may be obtained from local offices of the Department of Employment or from their headquarters in London. Leaflets and guidance on the Equal Pay Act and the Sex Discrimination Act may be obtained from the Equal Opportunities Commission. Guides to Pay as You Earn schemes may be obtained from any local office of the Inland Revenue, and leaflets concerning industrial injuries and supplementary benefits from local offices of the Department of Health and Social Security. Advice and publications on industrial relations matters may be obtained from the various regional offices of the Advisory, Conciliation and Arbitration Service (ACAS). Information relating to racial discrimination is available from The Commission for Racial Equality, Elliot House, and guidance on the requirements of the Health and Safety at Work etc. Act may be obtained from local offices of the Health and Safety Executive or from the Health and Safety Commission. Various inexpensive booklets on various aspects of personnel administration may be obtained from HMSO and other organisations. Appendix 3 contains the full addresses of the organisations mentioned in this paragraph.

Other aids to personnel managers which can be recommended are *Croner's Reference Book for Employers*, published by Croner Publications Limited, and *Employment Law Manual*, published by Gower Press. These books contain in easily understood form all legislation and regulations with which an employer must be familiar in respect of his responsibilities towards his employees. Subscribers receive a loose-leaf book containing current information which is kept up to date by means of an amendment service of revised and additional sheets.

1

The Purpose of a Personnel System

Every company has to develop a personnel information system to meet its own requirements. A system cannot simply be inserted into a company like a tape cassette and be expected to produce the desired results. It is necessary first to define what the system is intended to do, and then to examine what records and other paperwork are needed to achieve this.

Setting Objectives

The purpose of a system will vary enormously according to the objectives of the company and may well have to be decided by senior management and perhaps the board itself, leaving the application to the individual operating managers who will need to define their own information requirements within the broad framework of the overall objectives. These could be any of the following:

1 To support wage and salary administration
2 To facilitate selection and appointments
3 To help identify high-potential people
4 To determine in-company promotion
5 To help in the administration of management development and training programmes
6 To help develop the full potential of employees and departments

The objectives of a system will change in the process according to circumstances. In the past, for instance, determining wages has been the main purpose of employee information. Today, such things as records of skills for manpower planning have begun to assume equal importance.

There are legal constraints on a personnel information system. Every employer is compelled by law to complete forms and maintain records for government bodies, and this information must, of necessity, be an integral part of the documentation, and, indeed, may form the basis of individual forms. It is also essential as back-up material where cases of unfair dismissal, or sex or race discrimination, may arise.

Need for Analysis

Having established the purpose of a personnel information system, it is necessary to carry out a systematic analysis of existing procedures to identify the problems and the potential areas of improvement. One should know just what the personnel department is doing and how, what information is being provided and how it is used.

The procedures can be defined in very simple flow charts. Diagrams can be used to show the sequence of all the operations, movements and delays which occur in a procedure or series of procedures. They can also indicate the clerks who carry out each stage of the procedure and the equipment used. This is the clearest way of showing how one procedure affects another, the interaction of various forms, what information is copied from one form to another and what use is made of various copies.

It will not normally be feasible to start revising the entire system all at once. A situation where personnel records are being computerised may demand that the whole system be revised at one time, but this involves a lot of dislocation unless there already exists a very good system to serve as a basis. Perhaps the best approach is to start where there is a specific problem and to look at all the factors affecting it. If the cost of a large exercise needs to be justified, it may be preferable to start where there is likely to be the biggest payoff.

A senior manager, preferably a director, should be made responsible for the co-ordination of records, and one department should be responsible for keeping the essential records up to date, providing the information to others as a service and preparing the statistics needed. In larger companies, the personnel department is the most obvious choice. In smaller companies the department concerned with wages is most suitable.

Integrated Systems

Obviously there is a strong relationship between training, payroll and personnel records, and in smaller firms, in particular, a single data base is maintained. At first sight it may seem logical to want all information on employees in one place. An item of data would need to be entered only once, saving time in completing and processing separate records.

In practice, however, a single data base usually becomes too complex and impractical for a number of reasons. Different kinds of information are applicable to different tasks and serve different purposes. The purpose of a wages file, for example, is for paying, and the purpose of a personnel file is for providing information on employees. More often than not, data are collected, processed and reported quite independently of personnel department activities and information often cannot be supplied as needed by that department. Much of the personal data on payroll records do not directly affect the personnel department.

This does not mean, however, that forms cannot be designed to serve several functions. A form could be modified or combined with that of another department. In this way one form can perform a function which at present requires several forms.

Combining Forms

Clearly there must be a limit to the extent of records and forms used for obtaining, processing and reporting data. Some firms manage with remarkably few, but in most cases the paperwork is increasing at an enormous rate.

To regain control over the paper, one should begin by listing every form in use and its primary objective, the specific information it is intended to provide, or what action it is intended to facilitate, and its potential function. It may be useful to arrange all the data elements in a matrix to see the pattern of information gathered and disseminated. The following questions should be asked:

1 What is the function or purpose of this form?
2 Why is it necessary?
3 Is it worth what it costs to produce?
4 Can it be eliminated?
5 What is the worst thing that could happen if it were eliminated?
6 How else can its function be performed?
7 Could a rubber stamp, memo or entry on a chalkboard or chart be used instead?
8 What is the purpose of each copy?
9 Is each copy really needed?
10 Can it easily be kept up to date?
11 Could it be obtained easily from another source?

It may not be a bad idea, when carrying out an analysis of existing forms, to include in the inventory forms which are being stored. It may be that whole files of records are being stored because of one bit of information contained in them which could be included on some other record.

Design of Forms

The layout and design of personnel forms will depend very much on the procedures followed and the objectives of the information system. It is helpful if new forms are designed and old ones modified at the same time, particularly if forms are used in conjunction with others or if data are recorded from one to another, as in the case of application forms and personal history cards. In this case, relevant information should be in the same sequence and in similar locations on both documents, as far as this is possible.

The inclusion of every line, every entry, should be made to justify itself, although care must be taken not to exclude features which help to prevent constant queries.

The layout of the form should be clear, uncluttered, logical, easy to complete and easy to read. Ideally a form should be completed in natural sequence – from left to right and from top to bottom. Items which are always filled in are best located at the left of the form, items which are often completed in the middle and items which are seldom filled in at the right. This saves time when completing the form.

The main item of identification – the employee's name, for instance – should be wherever it can be most easily seen without drawing the entire form from the file. Filing margins where needed, pre-punched holes, a light rule to show where a form should be folded can all help in the disposition of forms.

As far as possible forms should be self-explanatory, especially those which are completed by people who are not employees – applicants and referees, for example. Specimen copies of each form should be kept in a special file, with details of how it is used, the supplier, the quantity ordered last with date, price and other relevant information. Notes of problems and ideas for improvement should be inserted as they come up so that they may be considered the next time the form is ordered. To facilitate re-ordering of forms, it is helpful to indicate on the foot of the last page of the form, in the smallest available type, the date, quantity and printer, together with the reference number of the document.

Legal Requirements

Whether or not an employer has a personnel department as such, he has certain legal obligations which must be fulfilled, even when only one person is employed.

Employers who intend to employ staff in an office or shop covered by the Offices, Shops and Railway Premises Act must complete Form OSR 1, illustrated in Figure 1:1. A separate form should be completed for each set of premises with a different postal address. Two copies must be completed and sent to the local authority (borough, urban district or rural district council; burgh or county council).

The Act also requires a fire certificate to be in force with respect to any premises to which the Act applies where more than twenty persons are employed to work at any one time or where more than ten persons are employed elsewhere than on the ground floor.

An employer must report to the local Inland Revenue office anyone whom he employs and is receiving £18.50 or more a week. It is also the employer's duty to deduct income tax from the pay of his employees whether or not he has been directed to do so by the tax office. If he fails to do this he may be required to pay over to the Inland Revenue the tax which he should have deducted and, in addition, may incur liability to penalties.

Changes in the way in which National Insurance contributions are calculated following the introduction of the State Pension Scheme in 1978 have given rise to the categorisation of employees into 'contracted out' or 'contracted in' – their status depends on the pension arrangements made by the employer. Special arrangements have been made for married women who have opted for a lower contribution rate with reduced benefits and for employees who continue to work after normal retirement age.

Further details as to the precise requirements may be obtained from the Department of Inland Revenue or the Department of Health and Social Security as appropriate.

General Register

The general register must be kept, in a form prescribed by The Factories Act General Register Order 1973, in every factory. Among other things, the register contains the prescribed particulars of the young persons employed in the factory, the prescribed particulars of every accident and case of industrial disease occurring in the factory, of which notice is required to be sent to a factory inspector, and particulars of every exception under the Act of which the occupier of the factory avails himself – in the employment of male young persons on shifts in certain industries, for example.

The occupier of a factory must send the factory inspector such extracts from the general register as the inspector may from time to time require in the execution of his duties. Under the regulations of the Disabled Persons (Employment) General Regulations 1944, employers who normally employ more than twenty people are required to employ a quota of registered disabled persons. It is advisable to identify personal records or to keep a separate list of employees who are registered disabled persons.

Overtime Reports

Employers must notify the district factory inspector of their intention to employ women and young persons over sixteen on overtime. For this reason it is essential that the personnel department, or whoever is responsible for notifying the factory inspector, be advised that overtime is being worked. In some cases a memorandum will suffice, but many firms have a specific form to ensure that all the information required is included.

Notices containing the prescribed particulars of such overtime must be posted in the factory and entered in the prescribed register in accordance with the Factories

Act 1961, Moreover, an employer is required by law to record all overtime work by women and young persons so that control can be exercised in accordance with the Factories Acts.

The personnel department must keep a record of all overtime hours worked. If work is carried out in accordance with the 'individual overtime regulations', a card must be kept for each person indicating the number of hours and the number of days that the person has worked overtime. It is helpful if this card has a built-in reminder for the personnel manager when the maximum number of hours or weeks that may be worked in a year is approached.

Public Notices

The following notices are required by the Factories Act to be displayed in every work room:

1 Hours and meal times
2 Any holidays substituted for statutory holidays
3 Address of the factory inspector and superintending inspector
4 Name and address of the employment medical adviser in charge of the area
5 The specific clock, if any, regulating the hours of work
6 The name of the person in charge of the first-aid box in every work room
7 The number of persons that can be employed in any work room
8 Prescribed abstract of the Act
9 Any special exceptions under sections 97–115 regarding factory hours which the company has been granted

Employers covered by the Employers' Liability (Compulsory Insurance) Act must keep copies of their certificate of insurance on display at each place of business throughout the period of insurance stated on the certificate.

In addition, other notices may be required to be displayed by legislation that applies to specific industries and particular types of factories. HMSO publish a list of such forms.

Holidays

There are in England eight 'customary' holidays:

> New Year's Day
> Good Friday
> Easter Monday
> The first Monday in May

The last Monday in May (Spring Holiday)
The last Monday in August (late Summer Holiday)
Christmas Day
Boxing Day (December 26, if it is not a Sunday)

In Scotland, New Year's Day and one other day are public holidays but Boxing Day and Easter Monday are not.

Women and people aged seventeen or less who are employed in factories must be given these customary holidays under the Factories Acts.

Other holidays, and entitlement to holiday pay, are fixed by individual or collective bargaining. In the industries that have them, wages councils regulate minimum holiday entitlement.

In principle, payment for holidays is the same as the amount that would have been paid had the employee worked for the holiday period.

Details of holiday entitlement must be given to employees in the statement required by the Employment Protection (Consolidation) Act, together with the method of calculation and payment and details of how entitlement is calculated in cases of termination (see page 49).

Figure 1:1   Registration form OSR1 (see facing page)
First page of the form that must be completed and sent to the appropriate authority
before employing persons to work in premises covered by the Offices, Shops and
Railways Premises Act. A separate form needs to be completed for each set of
premises with a separate postal address. Copies of this form can be obtained from the
district inspector of health and safety (Factory Inspectorate).

OFFICES, SHOPS AND RAILWAY PREMISES ACT 1963

Section 49 of the Offices, Shops and Railway Premises Act 1963, and the Notification of Employment of Persons Order 1964 require that if on the 1st May, 1964, you are employing, or are intending after that date to begin to employ, persons to work in shop or office premises other than certain offices occupied by railway undertakings (for definitions see notes 2 to 6 on pages 2 and 4), you shall complete this form and send it to the appropriate authority (see note 1). Persons who are already so employing staff on the 1st May, 1964, should delete Part I, complete Part III and send it off before 31st July, 1964. Persons who are intending to begin so to employ staff after 1st May, 1964, should delete Part II, complete Parts I and III, and send off the form before they first begin to employ staff.

Please ensure that the duplicate form on page 3 is completed (using carbon paper if you wish) and sent with the top copy to the appropriate authority. They will send the duplicate form to the fire authority for the area who also have duties in connection with the Act. (You may need a fire certificate if more than a certain number of people are employed in your premises—see note 8.)

A separate form should be completed for each set of premises with a different postal address. Where several occupiers have premises at the same address, each occupier should complete a form in respect of his premises.

Further notes will be found on pages 2 and 4 describing the classes of office and shop premises within the scope of the Act and indicating the appropriate authority to whom this form should be sent. You are advised to read these notes before you complete the form.

NOTICE IN FORM PRESCRIBED BY THE MINISTER OF LABOUR, OF EMPLOYMENT OF PERSONS IN OFFICE OR SHOP PREMISES

PART I

Notice is hereby given that on the _____ (*insert date*), the employer specified in Part III of this notice, will begin to employ persons to work in the premises described therein.

PART II

Notice is hereby given that the employer specified in Part III of this notice is employing persons to work in the premises described therein.

PART III

1. (*a*) Name of the employer ....

   (*b*) Trading name, if any ....

2. (*a*) Postal address of the premises ....

   ....

   (*b*) Telephone No. ....

3. Nature of business ....

4. How many persons are or will be employed by the employer in office or shop premises at the above address in the following types of workplace? (*See notes 3–7.*)

   (*a*) Office ....

   (*b*) Shop (retail) ....

   (*c*) Wholesale department or warehouse ....

   (*d*) Catering establishment open to the public ....

   (*e*) Staff canteen ....

   (*f*) Fuel storage depot ....

   TOTAL ....

   Of the TOTAL, how many are females? ....

5. How many of the total are or will be employed on floors *other* than the ground floor? ....

6. Of the total stated in reply to question 4, are any (or will any be) housed in separate buildings? (*Answer Yes or No*)...

7. Is the employer the owner of the building(s) (or part of the building(s)) containing the premises? (*Answer Yes or No*)...

8. If not, state the name and address of the owner(s) or person(s) to whom rent is paid ....

   ....

   Signature of employer or person authorised to sign on his behalf .... Date ....

For official use

2

Recruitment

In firms where there is little fluctuation in the volume of work to be performed it is often the practice simply to replace an employee who leaves. No authorisation is needed unless an increase in staff is required, in which case a requisition form should be raised, probably by the immediate supervisor, and authorised by a senior manager.

Employee Requisition Forms

In companies where close control is exercised, no new employee, whether a replacement or an addition, may be engaged without a requisition form which is scrutinised by the appropriate line manager before being passed on to the personnel manager for implementation. In many firms, decisions are made on a day-to-day basis by the responsible executive, according to business pressure or other immediate factors. In other firms, where the importance of manpower planning is realised, a definite establishment is determined for each department and a requisition form is considered according to a manpower plan.

A typical employee requisition form covers any or all of the following items:

1 Name of job
2 Rate of pay
3 Date by which new starter(s) required
4 Urgency of need
5 Whether additional or replacement (including name of person replaced)
6 Full time or part time
7 Day or shift work
8 Temporary (stating for how long) or permanent
9 Sex (if a genuine occupational qualification)

10 Age limits
11 A note of any special physical qualifications, such as strength, good eyesight, dexterity
12 Skill or experience
13 Special educational or similar requirements

The form should also bear the name of the department needing the labour and have spaces for the names of the person originating the form and the managers approving it, with routing directions.

The requisition forms can be clipped together to form a register of vacancies and be cancelled once the new starters are engaged. Some firms prefer to keep vacancies in a book register or to prepare an up-to-date list each week. The purpose of this is to see how long it is taken to fill requisitions in various categories; this information is necessary for manpower planning. A note on the requisition form of the source of recruits – such as the Department of Employment, newspaper advertisements, and so on – can be used to analyse the effectiveness of alternative recruitment methods.

Figures 2:1 and 2:2 are good examples of employee requisition forms. Figure 2:3 is a similar form designed for requisitioning staff.

Personnel Specifications

Initial selection is largely concerned with establishing an appropriate level of ability and aptitude for the post under consideration. The recruitment or selection procedure should be designed to achieve two basic aims:

1 To ensure that the level of ability of the candidate is in line with the requirements of the post or grade for which he is applying
2 To ensure as far as possible that the candidate's record of achievement and interests are likely to result in an equivalent performance within the recruiting organisation.

In most firms the personnel manager will have a good working knowledge of the requirements of most jobs. Where this is not so – in a very large organisation or one with a multiplicity of skills, for example – personnel specifications are necessary.

A personnel specification defines the kind of person needed for the job, the skills, knowledge, training and experience required to perform the job effectively and the worth of the job to the company – the salary. In this way it is possible to think in the same terms in assessing each candidate. This approach makes it easier to match candidates with particular vacancies and posts. It also forms a sound basis for developing a computer program for selection purposes.

In the past, most jobs have been classified as being done either by males or by females, but this ceases to be permissible under the Equal Pay Act. It may be, of course, that the physical demands of some jobs may preclude their performance by women. Equally the dexterity required for certain work prevents many men being effective performers. If the approach recommended here is used there should be no problems. The demands of the job are stated simply as physical requirements or limitations to be considered. They should not be barriers.

An example of a personnel specification is shown in Figure 2:4.

It is usually preferable to promote from within whenever possible, and most vacancies should be publicised internally unless special qualifications or experience are required. Such a policy ensures a cross-fertilisation of talent, develops every employee's potential, increases flexibility and demonstrates the company's concern for its employees. Apparent 'irreplaceability' in the present job should not be allowed to hinder promotion where this is deserved.

Many firms also keep a waiting list of applicants for various posts. Other firms, which have a number of suitable applicants for a particular post which is rarely vacated, keep surplus application forms for some time in case of a similar vacancy occurring. If the type of work for which the applicant is considered suitable is placed clearly on the front, and possibly at the top, of the form it will assist this type of filing.

Recruitment Advertisements

Equal opportunity legislation now makes it unlawful to publish or have published an advertisement which indicates an intention to discriminate by reason of sex, and this means that the use of certain job titles, such as salesgirl, postmen etc., could be taken as such an intention. This does not mean that these titles will disappear but it does mean that more care needs to be taken when drafting the necessary copy. (A Code of Practice on Advertising is now available from the Equal Opportunities Commission.)

A job description in an advertisement should contain specific duties and responsibilites and the salary range. Otherwise, it may lead to too many unsuitable applications and subsequent disenchantment of those attending interviews. Sometimes the firm is not identified and a box number is used instead. In many instances this is done because it is thought that if the firm's name appears too frequently the implication will be that it is unable to retain its employees. The great drawback of using a box number is that potential employees may fail to apply because they fear that it may be their own firm which is advertising.

In the case of staff advertisements, it often happens that a candidate sends a detailed curriculum vitae with his letter only to receive an application form requesting the same data. This duplication can be avoided by stating in the advertisement that the applicant should write in for an application form. Requests can be dealt with by a junior and the completed application form will present a more intelligible picture of the applicant. It may be advisable to state the job requirements more specifically, however, to reduce the number of unsuitable applicants.

Recruitment and advertising procedures often come under scrutiny and a sample form may be designed to help to identify the effectiveness of the advertisement and to monitor the system. Figure 2:5 is an example used to identify the number of replies to one particular advertisement and to monitor the progress of the interviewing procedure.

Application Forms

The application form is not only important in the selection procedure but also in providing information for the employee's file. The information contained in the application form is used as the basis for a personal record file. In some firms the application form is placed in a readily accessible position in the employee's file and serves as his personal history record. Little of the information on it needs to be transferred to other documents. The layout of the form must be specifically designed to fulfil this function, however.

In addition, the application form is useful in assisting interviewers, particularly departmental heads and line managers who have a limited knowledge of interviewing techniques.

The primary function of an application form, however, is for selection and it should be designed for this purpose. Essentially, the application should provide information needed by the employer to decide on the applicant's eligibility for a vacancy. In designing the form the whole range of jobs must be kept in mind. There is a wide variation between the information required from a prospective labourer and a skilled tool-maker and, on the staff side, between a clerk, an industrial nurse and a senior executive.

Figures 2:6 to 2:9 show some typical examples of application forms. Companies usually have different application forms for works and staff personnel. This is because more details are usually required of staff and also because works application forms are completed either in the waiting room, immediately before the interview, or during the interview, often by the interviewer. In the case of staff, the forms are usually completed at home and returned by post. Figure 2:10 illustrates an application form designed specifically for senior staff. The form shown in Figure 2:11 is used for all weekly and monthly paid staff, irrespective of level. A shorter form, shown in Figure 2:12, is used for office machine operators.

Some large firms also have separate forms for young people and apprentices. Greater space is devoted to school results, interests and ambitions and less space or none at all to previous jobs. Figure 2:13 is an example of a trainee application form.

Contents of application forms

What questions should be included on an application form? The possibilities are enormous and the variations almost infinite. An analysis of fifty application forms for manual workers resulted in a list of seventy questions, only four of which were common to all: name, address, date of birth and previous jobs. Few forms had more than twenty-five questions and probably many of the forms examined had not gathered sufficient information. Few firms, for example, were found to use the application form to ask where the vacancy was seen advertised. Thus most firms deny themselves the opportunity of assessing the various media used.

Every question included on an application form should help to screen, select or identify the candidate. Any other information, such as the applicant's religion, elementary education or the colour of his eyes, is questionable. It may also be questioned whether some of the information requested is really needed at this stage or if it would be better obtained at an interview. Any test of an applicant's enthusiasm or comprehension is best left to the interview. Personal questions which may be resented on a printed form should be avoided since they are likely to be answered more readily once friendly relations have been established at the interview. Other information which may not be required unless the applicant is accepted for employment should not be asked until then.

Needless to say, it is illegal to ask any questions to which the answers may be used to discriminate against an applicant because of sex, marital status, colour, race or nation of origin. It is also well to remember that certain questions need to be avoided in relation to the Rehabilitation of Offenders Act 1974. During recruitment an employer can ask a possible employee about conviction but under the Act he cannot ask about any 'spent' convictions or circumstances relating to a 'spent' conviction. It is also unlawful to discriminate against an employee because of a 'spent' conviction. All this type of information may well be needed for statistical analyses but it should not be used in any way which might reflect discrimination.

Items on an application form broadly fall into two categories. The first comprises those which identify the candidate, such as name, address and date of birth. It may be well to ask for both date of birth and age, incidentally. The age is more convenient to read but the date of birth is needed for personal records. This section can also include questions intended to elicit facts which might debar the applicant from employment, such as ill-health or age, or test the applicant's eligibility in accordance with company policy. These questions should be based upon an analysis of the work to be done.

The second section is normally used to record the applicant's qualifications, education, experience and personal qualities. Some firms prefer to limit their application forms to details of identification and have a supplementary form for this information which is completed during the interview. In this way confidential comments and tests results may be recorded and only the basic details of identification are given to personnel clerks for making up an employee's personal record card.

'Weighted' application forms are particularly useful for sales, executive and managerial positions. The weighted application is based on the results of an examination of the qualities of successful salesmen or executives employed by the firm. It thus indicates which qualities should be examined in depth.

The section of the form headed 'previous employment' is normally in reverse chronological order so that the applicant begins with his present or more recent job. If the interviewer wishes to go further back into the applicant's history, the other details will not be out of sequence.

A space for the candidate to cover any other points he feels relevant should be included on the form, especially on staff forms.

It is usual at the end of the form to add a statement, to be signed by the applicant, that the information given is a true and correct record. In some cases the statement continues with some such clause as: 'If accepted for employment I agree to abide by the terms and conditions laid down by the company.'

A section 'for office use only' can be used to record details of information which are required only if the applicant is engaged – such as his bank account number, for example.

Some employers ask for applications to be completed in handwriting, since handwriting is thought to be a useful indicator of fluency or personality. It would seem, however, that interpretations of handwritten applications seldom contain information detrimental to the applicant and the handwriting often makes it that much more difficult and time consuming to examine the candidate's qualifications.

Design and format of application forms

The importance of a well-designed application form is not always understood. Certain managements fail to appreciate the power of the application form to create an impression of the company which issues it. The quality of paper, printing and general layout has an obvious effect on the applicant. A badly designed and ill-considered application form can be damaging to a firm's reputation and can result in a poor selection of applicants for interviewing. As much attention should be paid to these forms as, say, to sales brochures and advertisements.

The format should be structured so that the information required for each department is together. It may even be practicable to include on the application form whole sections which would otherwise have to be maintained as separate forms, thus obviating the need for separate interview forms, medical examination reports, engagement forms, etc. If the application form is designed to complement the employees' personal records, the transfer of information from one to the other is made easier and the chance of error minimised. (See also the section on *Interview checklists*.)

Interviewing

Application forms alone are not sufficient to judge the suitability of candidates. In most cases, a member of the personnel department will interview prospective applicants and prepare a shortlist of applicants for the line manager or the immediate supervisor to see.

The application form can be useful at the interview, however. It gives the interviewer a preview of the shortlisted applicant, so that he can decide in advance what approach to use and on which areas he should concentrate. An interview is not for the purpose of asking an applicant questions which he has already answered on the application form. The interviewer's task is to assess the applicant's capability and competence, his potential, depth of knowledge, adaptability and probable impact on other employees.

Before the interview, the interviewer should consider the precise nature of the job to be filled and, if a personnel specification is not available, write down the qualities needed to carry out the job effectively. Different jobs call for different qualities. A research scientist need not make the same impact on others as does, say, a salesman.

If engagement is dependent upon a medical examination or security clearance the applicant should be informed of this fact at the interview.

Interview checklists

Most firms have some sort of interview checklist to assist the interviewer. A form which can be easily filled in by the interviewer reduces the need for note-taking which often disturbs the personal atmosphere, so conducive to a good interview. When a number of interviews take place in quick succession, an interview checklist helps to avoid questions being asked twice or forgotten altogether.

Many firms have a composite application form. The prospective applicant is asked to complete only the first part and the last part serves as an interview form or checklist. On the other hand, some firms prefer to limit their application forms to details for identification or which might debar the applicant from employment, using a separate or supplementary checklist to be completed during the interview. Confidential comments can then be recorded without becoming part of a permanent record.

Tests

The interview procedure may be supplemented by a test to determine the candidate's intelligence quotient and tests of specific aptitudes designed to assess the potentiality of the candidate for work involving special characteristics, such as mechanical aptitude, clerical aptitude, etc.

Letters requesting a candidate to attend an interview should state whether he will be taking any vocational or other tests. The interview programme can be arranged so that the individuals are interviewed in turn while others take tests. Candidates should be provided with the necessary paper, pencil and a copy of the day's programme.

One of the main uses of these specialised tests is to determine who is good enough for the job and who is too good for it. Where the candidate has no proven record of academic attainment or experience, tests provide an indication of the general level of ability and potential. In some instances, where a record of educational attainment is available, a marked discrepancy between test results and examination success or failure may warrant closer examination at the resulting interview.

There are other psychological tests of personality, creative ability and, more recently objective attainment, but in general these only apply to initial recruitment at a senior level.

Results of such tests must be interpreted against a person's background 'like a thermometer'. Because test administration and the interpretation of results require practice and an understanding of the underlying principles (not to mention the ethical implications) test results should normally be released only to those who have received adequate training in their use.

Reference Forms

An applicant is normally required by prospective employers to give the names and addresses of two or three persons, including his immediate superior in his present or more recent jobs, who may be referred to for information concerning his qualifications and character. It is doubtful, however, whether references are of much value and whether the time and effort spent by the personnel department in obtaining and supplying references is worth while.

The problem today is that, whilst the referee's position may be a responsible one and superior to the applicant's, his own competence and training may be less than that of the applicant and he may not be able to give a fair assessment or judgement. Moreover, employers in general are reluctant to write anything derogatory about even the most unsatisfactory employee.

The most feasible solution to this problem is for employers to indicate precisely the information sought. Basically a request for references should seek confirmation of statements made by the applicant and an objective appraisal of his personal characteristics. Letters requesting personal information should state the purpose of the letter, the information requested and express appreciation. They should be brief, specific and courteous. A former employer, for example, should be asked to confirm:

1 Employment dates
2 Nature of duties
3 Reason for leaving

The referee should also be asked to state the capacity in which he has known the applicant and the length of time.

A number of firms send a standard reference form which referees are asked to complete. Standard reference forms are usually preferred by referees as they indicate precisely the information required. At the same time, standard forms are useful in dissuading referees from making exaggerated comments and help to ensure a greater degree of accuracy and objectivity in comparing candidates. Figure 2:14 is an example of a reference form.

Below are typical questions asked in reference forms:

Earnings

His/her wages were £——per hour/week/month/year
Bonus

Health

How do you rate the applicant's health?
Very good/good/average/poor
Has he/she any physical defects?
If injured in your employ, please state nature of injury
Did applicant contract any industrial disease while in your service?
Are you paying compensation now?

Personal characteristics
1   Did you find the applicant to be strictly honest?
2   How do you rate the applicant in:
    (*a*) Ability
    (*b*) Character
    (*c*) Conduct
    (*d*) Accuracy
    (*e*) Cooperation
    (*f*) Time-keeping
3   Is there any other information which a prospective employer should know?
4   Is applicant free from engagement with you?

Open references should rarely be given by an employer, unless the employee is emigrating, as they are of little value to those who receive them. It should also be stressed that references given by one employer to another are intended to be treated in confidence and this should be stated in the request letter. They should not be filed with other personnel records where they can be seen by clerks, but locked with other confidential documents.

Figure 2:1   Employee requisition form

A type of requisition form used only for replacement of labour and thus tied in with the termination procedure. A coloured copy is retained by the departmental manager. The reverse side shows employees' names and starting dates.

TO PERSONNEL MANAGER		
EMPLOYEE REQUISITION		
No. required	Age range	Hours
Job	Qualifications and experience and any special circumstances	
Dept		
To commence		
Salary or wage		
I recommend the engagement/re-engagement of : Name _____ Address _____ _____ Green copy to be retained by Departmental Manager	Date	
	Signature Dept Manager	
	Approval	

Figure 2:2   Personnel requisition form (Twinlock Group)

Department_____ Date _____			

Date wanted	Number required	Job title	Wage/salary range	Suggested salary grade

Addition ☐   Permanent ☐   Male ☐   Normal hours ☐   Double day shift ☐

or   or

replacement ☐   temporary ☐   Female ☐   Day shift ☐   Night shift ☐

If temporary, for how long _____   Age limits   Special hours ☐

Person replaced, if replacement_____   Minimum_____

                                                       Maximum_____   Details

If addition to strength, give reason

Educational requirements   **Special educational requirements**

CSE ☐   Technical College ☐

GCE ☐   University ☐

_____ ☐   _____ ☐   Other requirements (eg Driving licence)

Do you know of anyone suitable for this position ?

Group personnel use only			
Number engaged	Response	Date requisition filled	

Department of Employment ☐   Journal group ☐   Recommended by_____
                                                                    (Supervisor filling form)

Youth Employment Service ☐   Weekly review ☐

Agencies ☐   _____ ☐   Authorised by _____
                                                                    (Manager)

Advertiser group ☐   _____ ☐   Authorised by _____
                                                                    (Director)

Filled from _____

Figure 2:3   Staff requisition form (Richard Costain Limited)

Please send to Personnel Department

Our reference _____

From _____ Department or Contract

The following staff is/are required and should be available

on/by the   19

Number required   Designation

Are/is required as additional to present strength
_____
                                    Qualifications

(*a*) Educational

(*b*) Technical or professional

(*c*) Special

(*d*) Practical experience

Age preferred   Salary proposed

Date _____   Signature _____

1 Description of work

2 Location

3 Physical conditions of job (*Only to be filled in if vacancy overseas*)

4 Living conditions (*Only to be filled in if vacancy overseas*)

5 Any other points which might help in selecting suitable candidate

Figure 2:4   Personnel specification
Any one of the qualifications could be broken down into more specific requirements. For example, item 6 under "experience" could specify experience in the use and construction of PERT networks, in the use of Gantt charts, in the use of mathematical techniques to determine optimum batch size, and of administering production control schemes.

Title of post Project leader: Hydraulic engineering systems
Age range   25–35
Qualifications Degree or HNC in mechanical engineering. Endorsement in electrical
                  engineering desirable
Salary range £4500 to £5500 on appointment

Related industrial experience

Previous experience within the aircraft industry manufacturing hydraulic components desirable, preferably not less than three years or more than five years since completion of initial training.

Related experience in manufacturing hydraulic components for mining or other industries would be acceptable, preferably not less than three years, and nor more than five years. Similar period of related experience in manufacturing general engineering components would be useful.

Organisational consideration

A candidate preferred who has worked in a medium-sized organisation (between 400 and 1500 employees) – an appreciation and understanding needed of the kind of management services, structure and authority appropriate to organisations of this size.

Breadth of experience

Knowledge and experience of the following activities necessary

1   Design of hydraulic equipment
2   Testing of hydraulic equipment
3   Assembly of hydraulic equipment
4   Quality control of hydraulic equipment
5   Control of manufacture of hydraulic equipment
6   Experience as project leader in charge of hydraulic equipment
7   Design and manufacture of electro-mechanical systems

Figure 2:5   Progression of recruitment procedure form

This analyses the source of applicants and monitors the progress of each applicant through the procedure (Greater London Council)

ADVERT NO: _____   CLOSING DATE: _____

JOB DESCRIPTION NO: _____

NO.	NAME	DATE SENT	WHICH PAPER?	DATE ACK.	HOLDING LETTER	COMMENTS

Figure 2:6   Application form
This is the first page of a four-page application form. The remaining pages cover positions held, references, foreign languages, spare-time activities, space for additional information from the applicant, interview notes and conditions of employment

APPLICATION FOR EMPLOYMENT		
Surname	Forenames	

Date of birth		Height	Married/single/widowed	Nationality

| Date of birth of children | Boys | | | |
| | Girls | | | |

Address	Telephone No

Health (mention any disability, serious illness or operation which you have had)

Are you prepared to undergo a medical examination ?	Name and address of Doctor	Are you a registered disabled person
Have you been previously employed or refused employment by this company ?	Are you related to, or do you know anyone in our employ ?	No of certificate if registered

Next of kin
(Name and address)

Position now desired	Salary expected	Notice required by present employer

SCHOOL RECORD

Names of schools attended	Dates	Scholarships won, examinations passed with subjects taken	Dates

FURTHER EDUCATION

University, technical college, evening classes, institutes, etc	Courses or subjects studied	Diplomas, certificates, etc	Dates

School/college offices held, part taken in games, societies, other activities

Figure 2:7 Application form

The first and last pages of the form are shown. The whole of one of the centre pages is for the use of the interviewer; the other is for details of present and previous employment and supplementary information

PERSONAL DETAILS		
Surname	Forenames	
Present address and permanent address if different		Phone number
Age / Date of birth	Place of birth	Married or single
Nationality	Nationality at birth	Surname at birth (if different)
Next of kin / Forenames / Surname / Address	Relationship / Nationality at birth / Surname at birth	Dependants

EDUCATION AND TRAINING					
	Name and type	From	To	Main subjects studied	Degrees, diplomas and certificates
School(s) from age eleven					
University or technical college (full time)					
Part time education					
Membership of technical or professional associations					

Figure 2:7 *continued*

For use by the company	MEDICAL OFFICER	

Recommendations

Signed: Date:

ENGAGEMENT

Starting date	Department			

Job

Grade	Salary	S/R	Hours	SC/non SC

Name and address of bank (if any)

Special comments

Departmental head	Date
Personnel officer	Date

Figure 2:8   Application form

Surname Mr Mrs Miss	Position applying for

Other names	How did you hear of us? Give name of newspaper, etc

Address	Date of birth	Place of birth

	Nationality	Marital status

Telephone number

Name and address of next of kin	Forenames and dates of birth of children under nine years of age				

Telephone number	Is there someone to mind the children?

Names of friends or relatives with company	

If you have previously had employment with the company, give name of department, dates and reason for leaving	

Disabilities (if any)	Registration number

Have you ever suffered from

Chest complaints?	When?
Dermatitis?	When?
Diabetes?	When?
Epilepsy?	When?

Have you ever received compensation under the Industrial Injuries Acts?

Have you ever had any serious illness (other than those mentioned above) or operation?

Figure 2:8 *continued*

EDUCATION			
Secondary, public or grammar school	From	To	Details of exam results
Further education (Day or evening technical college, postal course, etc)	From	To	Details of exam results, courses taken or being taken
Details of apprenticeship or training received			
Have you any other skills or abilities which might interest us? (eg Foreign languages, mechanical aptitude, etc)			
Membership of professional bodies, unions, etc			

PREVIOUS EMPLOYMENT				
Name and address of present or last employer	Job	Rates/wages	Dates	

Dates of service in HM forces—from   to

Branch or regiment   Trade   Last rank

It is understood that you may apply for references from my present
and previous employers, prior to engagement   Signed _____

It is also understood that, should I take up employment with the company,
wages are paid on Fridays for work completed the previous Friday   Date _____

Personnel department use only
Interviewed by
Remarks

Figure 2:9   Application form (Marconi Company Limited)

The Marconi Company Limited
APPLICATION FOR EMPLOYMENT

FORENAMES (BLOCK LETTERS)	SURNAME (BLOCK LETTERS)

TEMPORARY ADDRESS	PERMANENT ADDRESS
SINCE: TEL. No.:	SINCE: TEL. No.:

GIVE ANY ADDRESS OUTSIDE U.K. USED WITHIN LAST THREE YEARS (EXCEPT HOLIDAYS) WITH DATES:

SURNAME AT BIRTH IF DIFFERENT	PRESENT NATIONALITY	DATE OF BIRTH
NATIONALITY AT BIRTH	TOWN AND COUNTRY OF BIRTH	

SINGLE	ENGAGED	MARRIED	FULL NAME OF SPOUSE
		CHILDREN	

SURNAME OF SPOUSE AT BIRTH	DATE OF MARRIAGE	NATIONALITY AT BIRTH	TOWN AND COUNTRY OF BIRTH

EDUCATION	DATES	EXAMINATIONS AND RESULTS	DATES
SECONDARY SCHOOLS			
UNIVERSITY/COLLEGE			

WHAT SORT OF POSITION ARE YOU SEEKING ?

WHEN ARE YOU AVAILABLE TO JOIN THIS COMPANY ?

PLEASE COMPLETE IF YOU ARE UNDER 21 OR IF EITHER PARENT IS OF FOREIGN ORIGIN:

MOTHER'S FULL NAME	FATHER'S FULL NAME
MOTHER'S SURNAME AT BIRTH	FATHER'S SURNAME AT BIRTH

NATIONALITY	TOWN AND COUNTRY OF BIRTH	NATIONALITY	TOWN AND COUNTRY OF BIRTH

PARENTS' PRESENT ADDRESS

SINCE:

004/06221

Figure 2:9 *continued*

Date Joined	Date Left	RECORD OF EMPLOYMENT	SALARY
		EMPLOYER, POSITIONS HELD, RESPONSIBILITIES, ETC	

APPLICANTS SIGNATURE: DATE

TO BE COMPLETED BY INTERVIEWER

PLACE	DATE	INTERVIEWER

ACTION

A GEC-Marconi Electronics Company   PRIVATE AND CONFIDENTIAL

Figure 2:10   **Application for for senior staff** (Williams Lea Limited)

---

1 Personal details _____
   Full name _____
   Address _____
   _____ Telephone _____
   Next of kin and address _____
   _____ Telephone _____
   Date of birth _____ Marital status _____ Nationality _____
   Number of children _____ Ages _____ Husband's/wife's occupation _____
   Are you registered disabled _____ Have you had any serious illness in the past five years _____
   Do you have a valid car driving licence _____

2 Position applied for _____
_____

3 Educational record

Secondary education Name of school	From	To	Examinations taken, detailing subjects passed and any special achievements

Further education University or colleges attended	From	To	Details of examinations passed and any special achievements

Technical or professional training Apprenticeship, course, college, institute	From	To	Examinations passed, qualifications and any special achievements

4 Record of previous employment
Start with your present job and work backwards
including any service with HM Forces

Employer's name and address	From	To	Position held, who you reported to and for whom you were responsible and a brief summary of job content	Starting and finishing salary	Reasons for leaving

Figure 2:10 *continued*

5 Any foreign languages?
If so, which and what proficiency? _____

_____

6 Any other information that you would
like to give about yourself or your experience

_____

7 Do you have any major leisure interests?

_____

8 May we contact any of your previous employers? Yes/No *
If yes, please give below the names and telephone
numbers of any of your past immediate managers   *Delete inappropriate
with whom we may speak about you   No approach will be made to your present employers at this stage

Name and position   Company and telephone number

9 If selected, when could you start? _____

10 Name and address of any referees
One should be from within your existing company and one
from outside your family who has known you at least five years
Name _____
Address _____
Name _____
Address _____

11 I certify that the information given is a true record and, if   Signature
selected, I agree to abide by the terms and conditions laid down
by the company   Date

Interview assessment rating (for office use only)

Code	1.5	6.10	11.15	16.20	Total	Remarks
WH1						
WH2						
WH3						
WH4						
WH5						
WH6						
WH7						
AP1						
PE 1						
PE 2						
PE 3						
PE 4						
PE 5						
PE 6						
PE 7						
PE 8						
SO1						
SO2						
SO3						
SO4						

Assessment total   Total percentile rating

Short listed _____
Referees checked _____
Commencing date _____
Commencing salary _____
Date offer made _____
Date offer accepted _____

Interviewed by _____ at _____ Date _____
Interviewed by _____ at _____ Date _____

Figure 2:11 Application form for staff
This form is used in connection with all weekly and monthly paid staff irrespective of level (Richard Costain Limited)

Application for employment as _____

I PERSONAL PARTICULARS _____

Surname _____

Forenames _____

Present address _____

_____

Permanent address (if different)_____

_____

Telephone number_____   Date of birth _____

Nationality_____   Marital status _____

Number, age and sex of children _____

Name of next of kin _____   Relationship_____

Address _____

_____

Occupation _____

Health *Have you ever suffered from any serious disease or disability? If so please give details (Give*

RDP number if appropriate) _____

_____

_____

Hobbies or leisure pursuits _____

2 EDUCATION

Name and type of secondary schools attended

_____ From _____ to _____

_____ From _____ to _____

_____ From _____ to _____

Examinations passed (please give details)_____

_____

_____

Figure 2:11 *continued*

Further education colleges and universities attended

_____ From _____ to _____

_____ From _____ to _____

Examinations passed (for degrees, please give subject and details) _____

_____

Professional qualifications _____

_____

_____

Knowledge and standard of foreign languages spoken _____ _____

3 EMPLOYMENT RECORD

Employment record, including service in HM Forces, commencing with present employer
(please use separate sheet of paper if necessary)

Name and address _____

_____

Date, salary and job title on joining _____

Current salary _____ Length of notice required _____

Present job title _____

Reason for wishing to leave _____

Name and address _____

_____

Date, salary and job title (*a*) on joining _____

(*b*) on leaving _____

Reason for leaving _____

Figure 2:11 *continued*

Name and address _____

_____

Date, salary and job title (*a*) on joining _____

(*b*) on leaving _____

Reason for leaving _____

Name and address _____

_____

Date, salary and job title (*a*) on joining _____

(*b*) on leaving _____

Reason for leaving _____

Name and address _____

_____

Date, salary and job title (*a*) on joining _____

(*b*) on leaving _____

Reason for leaving _____

Please list all training courses attended of over one week's duration including details of any apprenticeships served

Please give full postal addresses of 3 persons or companies to whom reference may be made (Business references preferred)
NB your present employers will not be approached without your permission

Name and address _____

_____

Name and address _____

_____

Name and address _____

_____

Figure 2:11 *continued*

Please give any other relevant particulars about your career

Signed   Date

Please return to   Reference number

Figure 2:12 Application form for office machine operator (Richard Costain Limited)

---

3 EMPLOYMENT RECORD

If applying for secretary/typist position give your current speed

Shorthand_____words per minute   Typing_____words per minute

If applying for machine operator position, state types of machine and length of experience

_____

Employment record commencing with present employer. Two or more previous employers will be asked to give references, but your present employer will not be approached without your permission

Name and address _____

_____

Current salary (including bonus and luncheon vouchers) and position _____

_____ Notice required _____

Name and address _____

_____

Date, salary and position on joining and leaving _____

_____

Name and address _____

_____

Date, salary and position on joining and leaving _____

_____

Name and address _____

_____

Date, salary and position on joining and leaving _____

_____

Signed _____ Date _____

Please return to   Reference number

For office use only			
Position	Commencing salary	Date started	Source of recruitment

Figure 2:13 Application form for trainees (Richard Costain Limited)

Application for training as _____

I PERSONAL PARTICULARS

Surname _____

First names _____

Present address _____

_____

Permanent address (if different) _____

_____

Telephone number_____   Date of birth_____

Nationality _____   Marital status _____

Name of next of kin _____   Relationship _____

Address _____

_____

Occupation _____

Health. *Have you ever suffered from any serious disease or disability ? If so please give details*

_____

_____

Interests. *Please give any information about yourself which you feel would be relevant to your application. Include details of any vacation work*

Figure 2:13 *continued*

---

2 EDUCATION

Please list name and type of schools, colleges or universities attended

_____ From _____ to _____

_____ From _____ to _____

_____ From _____ to _____

_____ From _____ to _____

Examinations taken Please list subjects taken, dates, examining body, results and grades obtained

Examinations to be taken

Please give full postal addresses of 2 persons to whom references may be made (One should be your housemaster or headmaster)

Name and address _____

_____

Name and address _____

_____

Signed _____ Date _____

Please return to _____ Reference number _____

Figure 2:14 Reference form

Dear Sir,

     The above –named has applied to this company for employment as a _____

and states having been in your service as _____ from _____

to _____ Clock number was _____

     We shall be greatly obliged if you will kindly confirm this and answer the questions detailed over, concerning the applicant. A stamped addressed envelope is enclosed for your reply which will be treated in strict confidence.

                                                    Yours faithfully,

When did applicant enter your employment ?	
When did applicant leave your employment ?	
Was employment continuous during this period ?	
Reason for leaving ?	
In what capacity was applicant employed by you ?	
At what salary or wage ?	
Has applicant given satisfaction in the following: *(a)* Conduct *(b)* Honesty *(c)* Workmanship *(d)* Timekeeping *(e)* Sobriety	
Was general health good ?	
Did applicant receive any injury while in your employ ? If so, please state nature of accident	
Has applicant at any time received, or is applicant at present in receipt of, compensation ?	
Is applicant to your knowledge registered under Disabled Persons (Employment) Act ?	
Did you receive a reference with this person ? If so, from whom?	

General remarks :

Date _____   Signature _____

                                                  Designation _____

3

Employment Forms

When an applicant has been selected for employment this must be communicated to everyone concerned within the company. In many instances a standard form is issued by the personnel department to advise the wages, medical and other departments concerned, and at the same time to remind the supervisor or departmental head of the starting date. Figure 3:1 is an example of such a form.

It may be, however, that the supervisor or departmental head has not only participated in the selection of the new employee but has the final say in the choice. In these circumstances, standard forms (Figure 3:2) are completed by the supervisor or the departmental head to inform the personnel department that a candidate has been engaged.

When an applicant is accepted, it is normal to send a letter which formally offers the appointment and which briefly sets out details of the main terms and conditions of employment. The wording of such a letter is clearly of consequence as it will normally be legally binding. Although the Employment Protection (Consolidation) Act requires that a written statement of terms and conditions be issued to all employees within thirteen weeks of their engagement, various terms become effective immediately or within four weeks and it is now common practice to enclose a written statement or a printed handbook setting out works or staff conditions of employment.

In certain cases, the letter is used to remind the new employee where, when and to whom to report. It should also indicate any documents, such as a birth certificate, which should be brought with him and it is advisable to ask the applicant to inform the employer whether or not he accepts the offer.

Induction Procedures

A new employee arriving on his first day of work should be asked by the personnel department or his immediate supervisor to hand over parts 2 and 3 of certificate P45, which he should have received from his previous employer. The new employer keeps part 2 and sends part 3 of the P45 (Figure 3:3) to the tax office and prepares a weekly or monthly deduction card for the employee.

If the new employee is starting his first job, or has lost the form, or is unwilling to produce parts 2 and 3 of his P45 for any reason – he may not wish to disclose his previous earnings – the new employer must complete Form P46 (Figure 3:4) which is then sent to the tax office. He must also prepare a deduction card and deduct income tax from the employee's pay, according to the emergency card tables, until a code number has been notified by the tax office. If the employee has been earning less than £18.50 a week in his previous employment, there will be no code on his P45 and a code number will have to be obtained. If the employee is known to have another job, the employer need not prepare a deduction card: the tax office will issue it.

It is advisable to ask a new employee to produce his birth certificate (a passport will do) to verify his age for insurance and pension purposes. It may sometimes be desirable, incidentally, to check his education certificates.

Induction checklist

An induction checklist (Figures 3:5 and 3:6) is intended to serve as a reminder of all forms that must be raised and action which must be taken when a newcomer starts his employment. The checklist is sometimes a separate document, but sometimes appears on the application form.

The checklist normally consists of items or boxes to be ticked or initialled as each procedure is completed. These may include the following:

1   Collection of tax form P45, or raising of the temporary coding form
2   Checking birth certificates, educational certificates, union membership card and references
3   Signing deduction-from-wages form
4   Checklist of forms raised for new starters
5   Entry made in journal or day book
6   Issue of employee handbook, gate pass, protective clothing, instruction manuals, equipment, identification badge or pass

Some firms also find it worth while to have a brief checklist to be used by the new employee's supervisor or the personnel department for follow-up of the new employee one month or three months after the start of his employment. The date of the follow-up interview can be inserted on the follow-up form when the employee first starts and the form kept in date order ready for the appointed day. Alternatively, dates can be raised each week from the journal entries of one or three months previously. The completed form bearing the interviewer's comments can be kept in the employee's file.

Application to Refund Tax

If the tax tables show that a refund exceeding £50 is due to a new employee on his first day, the employer enters the amount repayable in column 7 of the deduction card, completes form P47 (Figure 3:7) and sends it to the tax office. Refund should be made only on receipt of the authority from the tax office on form P48.

Tax deductions on the second and subsequent pay days should proceed as though the refund had actually been made, and any refund which may become due on those pay days should be made whether or not the authority from the tax office to make the refund due on the first pay day has been received.

Work Permits

Commonwealth citizens and aliens (other than nationals of countries in the European Economic Community) who wish to enter the United Kingdom in order to take employment will normally have to have a work permit. These are issued by the Department of Employment, Commonwealth Immigration Section or Foreign Labour Section, Ebury Bridge House, Ebury Bridge Road, London SW1W 8PY.

An exception to this rule is that Commonwealth citizens with a parent or grandparent born in the United Kingdom will not have to obtain a work permit, but they must hold an entry clearance certificate issued by the British Embassy or High Commission in their Commonwealth country of birth.

Applications for work permits may be made only by employers and will have to satisfy a number of conditions concerning age, skill and experience and the availability of resident workers in the United Kingdom or countries of the EEC. A work permit will be issued only for a specific job with a specific employer and for a maximum period of 12 months. Extensions of stay may be granted by the Home Office if the permit holder subsequently remains in approved employment, and, after four years in approved employment, application can be made for the entry conditions to be removed. Changes of employment will require the approval of the Department of Employment and this will be given subject to the satisfaction of the normal conditions for the issue of work permits.

Commonwealth citizens and aliens who do not have work permits and who are allowed to enter the United Kingdom on other than employment grounds must apply, in the first instance, to the Home Office, Immigration and Nationality Department, Lunar House, Wellesley Road, Croydon CR9 2BY for a variation of entry conditions if they wish to take employment. If the Home Office agree, they must then obtain the approval of the Department of Employment before commencing work.

As nationals of EEC countries enjoy complete freedom of movement in all EEC countries they do not require permits to work in the United Kingdom.

A firm or organisation wishing to offer a period of training for a limited period to a

Commonwealth citizen who is subject to employment control should submit an application on the prescribed form which can be obtained from any Job Centre or employment office.

There are special arrangements for the issue of permits for foreign nationals who are to be attached to British firms in a supernumerary capacity.

Issue Forms

It is usual for the employee to be requested to sign a form for any protective clothing, equipment or any identification card issued to him. This receipt should be filed in his personal file, and returned to him when he terminates employment or when any of these are returned to the company. If any goods are not returned the cost can be reclaimed in the same way as an ordinary debt. That is, it cannot be deducted from his wages, but must be paid separately. (See Truck Acts 1831–1940.)

Each employee can be asked for a deposit, but there can be no compulsion. Similarly, it would be inadvisable to compel an employee to purchase any equipment. But if it is purchased, it is unwise to deduct the cost from wages. It should be purchased outright by the company and the employee should repay them in instalments, independent of wages.

No charge can be made for equipment which the employer is compelled by law to provide.

Registration of Private Vehicles

The increasing number of cars and motor cycles which employees bring into factories is creating problems that are often left to the personnel department to handle. If the number of vehicles is limited, a pass with authorisation to park on company premises should be issued to the new employee, and the pass number recorded on his file.

It would not be unreasonable, incidentally, to insist that an employee should provide his own insurance against any damage to his vehicle while on company premises. If the company has arranged to cover itself it might be necessary to record each motor car and cycle. Alternatively, an insurance company could be asked to consider a group scheme for motor car insurance up to a given aggregate value and the premium might be met by a contributory scheme, the employee's contribution being assessed on the value of his car.

Contracts of Employment

The Employment Protection (Consolidation) Act 1978 requires all employers to issue a written statement of the basic terms and conditions of employment to all new employees who work more than a certain number of hours per week not later than thirteen weeks after the beginning of their employment. The Act does not, however, undermine the employer's or employee's right to create and determine such contracts. The terms of employment are agreed between the employer and employee, and in only one area, that of notice of termination, does the Act provide for minimum requirements. The contract itself is not required by law to be in writing but the Act does lay down certain requirements in relation to the written statement of terms and conditions of employment.

The wording to be used in the statement is left to the discretion of each firm in accordance with its policy and practice but what is required is that each employee should be fully aware of his terms of engagement, what is expected of him and what he is entitled to by virtue of his employment. The particulars to be included are:

1 Name and address of employer
2 Name and address of employee
3 Title of the job which the employee is employed to do
4 Date when employment began
5 Date of commencement of employment with a previous employer which counts as continuous employment
6 The scale or rate of remuneration or the method of calculating remuneration
7 The intervals at which remuneration is paid
8 Normal hours of work
9 Any terms and conditions relating to hours of work
10 Arrangements for overtime if worked
11 Terms and conditions relating to holidays and holiday pay, including sufficient information to enable the employee's entitlement (including entitlement to accrued holiday pay on termination) to be precisely calculated
12 Terms and conditions relating to incapacity for work because of sickness or injury, including provisions for sick pay and action to be taken by the employee
13 Pension and pension schemes
14 Length of notice which the employee is obliged to give and entitled to receive
15 (a) Disciplinary rules applicable or reference to a document which is reasonably accessible

(b) a person to whom the employee can apply if dissatisfied with any disciplinary action
16 Procedure for dealing with grievances
17 Existence of any closed shop agreement

In each case, where there are no particulars to be given, the written statement must say so. For all or any of the particulars except 15(b) and 16 the written statement may refer the employee to a document or documents which he has reasonable opportunities of reading in the course of his employment, or which are made accessible to him in some other way. If all or any of the terms of employment are set out in a collective agreement an employer may refer an employee to a copy of this. Other documents which might be used in the same way are works handbooks, wages regulation orders, booklets about sick-pay schemes or pension schemes and notices about such things as works holidays.

Figure 3:8 shows a typical statement of terms and conditions.

If there is a change in the terms of employment the employer must inform the employee about it not more than one month after by means of a further written statement or by providing an up-to-date reference document. A notice of change on bulletin boards will be sufficient if the employee is advised in advance of this procedure. A written statement notifying the employee of any such change may also specify the date on which his continuous period of employment began.

Employee Handbooks

There are, in fact, many other matters which it would be useful for employees to know and many firms incorporate this information, including the statement of terms of employment, into a handbook. Such a handbook is a useful part of an induction scheme, but it should not be a substitute for a proper introduction procedure.

An employee handbook may be intended merely to welcome and inform a new employee. Occasionally, handbooks are designed to fit in with recruitment policies as well. The handbook may serve as a manual of standard operating procedures for all employees, in which case it will be necessary to allow for changes to be inserted. A loose-leaf booklet may be the best solution. Moreover, a loose-leaf binder can also cater for a great variety of types and levels of new employees with special pages for works employees, weekly-paid people, apprentices and management. In the long run, loose-leaf binders are cheaper to produce since single pages with new information can be printed separately.

Pocket-size booklets, though usual, are not necessarily the most suitable. In the first place, it is doubtful whether handbooks are really kept in pockets. A larger format allows illustrations to be displayed to better advantage. Some booklets have pockets at the back for other papers, such as details of the pension scheme or sick and benevolent fund. Most have a perforated slip to be signed by the new employee, signifying that he has received the book and accepts the terms and conditions of employment. This acknowledgement can then be kept in the employee's file. Most employee handbooks contain:

1 An introduction by the chief executive
2 A short account of the company's history and its products or services
3 An organisation chart
4 Conditions of employment
5 Statement of company's safety policy
6 Training (including works rules)
7 Receipt for handbook

Introduction

This should set out the purpose of the handbook and include a brief general policy statement. It must, by law, outline particular positive features of the company's personnel policy (Safety, Non-discrimination etc.). The introduction should end with a brief statement to the effect that the company tries to provide challenge and opportunities at work to all, regardless of sex, race or religion and hopes that the employee will take advantage of them.

The flavour should be that of a convincing message of welcome – not easy to achieve. A high moral tone should be avoided, otherwise the picture created will probably be false.

Company history

This should be kept as short as possible and it is best restricted to important dates, perhaps illustrated with small drawings depicting company products.

Organisation charts

A brief explanation of how the company is owned and financed can be included as most employees do not normally have access to this kind of information.

An organisation chart showing other departments helps them to see where they fit into the overall structure, and a simple map showing various departments is useful to help them settle into their new environment.

Conditions of employments

This should be the central section of the handbook and it is essential that it is well laid out and divided into sections which are clear and logical.

Factors included may well be those referred to in the section on Contracts of Employment but other relevant items would be statements on Personnel and Industrial Relations Policy and Procedures, Security of Employment, and finally benefits, services and facilities.

Safety

This section must by law include a statement of company policy and remind employees of their general responsibilites for safety both to themselves and to their colleagues. It could include such items as:

i)   general safety regulations
ii) special hazards
iii) safety committee – its composition and function

    iv)   traffic regulations on company premises
     v)   smoking – areas where this is forbidden
    vi)   fire – notification and procedures
   vii)   provision of safety clothing
  viii)   first aid – location of boxes, surgery etc.
    ix)   procedure for reporting accidents

Training

The statement on training is very important and should reflect the company's approach to the development of the individual regardless of sex, age or race – the possibilites for promotion and advancement.

Receipt for handbook

Although it is not a legal requirement, a written receipt for a company handbook can be useful in situations where a company needs to prove that it has supplied certain information e.g. claims of unfair dismissal, breach of safety regulations etc.

The format can be quite simple and need only include the name and address of the employee, the date of entering employment, and the date of signature after reading and acceptance.

Personnel Records

It is essential for an employer to have a current record of the entire workforce. He must know, for example, the number and type of people in his employment in order to calculate his payments for National Insurance Contributions and his contribution to the Redundancy and Maternity Funds, and to provide information to the relevant Industrial Training Board. In addition the employer needs certain basic information about each employee.

This is a task which offers no technical problems and merely requires systematic listing of employees. It is advisable to identify records or to keep a separate list of all employees under the age of eighteen as their employment is regulated by law.

In addition to each employee's name, an employer should record his address, his position in the company, his date of birth and his National Insurance number. It is also a good idea to record the sex of the employee, as sickness and retirement benefits for women differ from those for men.

It is also necessary to know the date of engagement, as an employee's years of service may be a factor in calculating his wages or compensation under the Redundancy Payments Act. The date is also required on the written statement of terms and conditions of employment. Age may also affect an employee's claim to redundancy payments. Employees under eighteen and over sixty-five (sixty for women) are not entitled to a redundancy payment under the Employment Protection (Consolidation) Act. If a man's contract terminates when he is between the ages of sixty-four and sixty-five his redundancy compensation is reduced by one-twelfth for every complete month by which his age exceeds sixty-four. In the case of women, one-twelfth is deducted for every complete month by which their age exceeds fifty-nine. The simplest and cheapest filing system available is the ordinary card index box which can be kept on a desk top or in a desk drawer. The cards themselves are stiff enough to withstand frequent handling but flexible enough to be inserted in a typewriter. They are available in different colours which can be used to identify the various categories of employees.

Rotary wheels are useful where there is a large number of index cards which are referred to frequently. The cards are secure and do not fall out when the wheel is revolved, although they can be easily removed and replaced.

Pre-printed card strips (Figure 3:9) designed for personnel offices are available from Kalamazoo Limited, Birmingham, for inserting in binders. These card strips are available in five colours and sizes and are thin enough to be inserted in a typewriter for recording personal details.

Larger personnel cards for recording a greater amount of detail are also available and can be filed so that they overlap, showing only the bottom edge containing the most significant information (Figure 3:10).

Labour Analyses

Periodic and systematic analyses of the personnel records are important. Such analyses show the composition of the labour force and are useful indicators of the firm's growth. An analysis will indicate trends in the labour situation. This is particularly important for manpower planning, training and development programmes.

An inventory may show, for example, shortages of skilled manpower in some areas and surpluses in others. This will indicate a need to recruit labour in specific categories or trades, although the total labour requirements of the company as a whole may be decreasing. There may also be a possibility of balancing labour requirements within the company by transfer between departments, or other companies, of surplus labour in certain categories or trades.

An inventory of labour also provides the necessary details needed to complete returns for the Department of Employment, employers' federations and trade associations, and any reports should be presented in such a way that they facilitate the preparation of these returns. The number of those who have joined and left within a twelve-month period expressed as a percentage of the average labour strength is a useful measure of effective selection and induction methods.

Methods of analysis

Labour analyses will vary according to the nature of the firm, but a typical analysis would contain numbers according to department, indicating whether they are direct or indirect workers, and be divided by trade or skill groups. Employees could be identified as skilled, semi-skilled, trainees, apprenticed, administrative, executive, supervisory or clerical, for example. If appropriate, the numbers of temporary or part-time workers, disabled persons or shift workers are also shown.

Reports produced by the personnel department usually give a breakdown by department and location of the following information for both male and female employees:

1   Average number employed
2   Starters
3   Leavers
4   Turnover percentage
5   Length of service
6   Reason for leaving

Further breakdowns in the returns, such as by age, sex, and specific skills, are advisable, but these are usually reported annually. The main purpose of an age breakdown is to check whether there is any category of employees who are all of the same age. If there is, a replacement problem will arise when the group reaches retirement age and early steps should be taken to ease or avoid this difficulty. An overall appraisal of the age pattern is also necessary in the event of any proposed revision or rationalisation of various pensions schemes.

The ratio of direct to indirect workers is maintained in some firms, although the results are meaningless unless the firm's practice remains constant. An accurate calculation of particular union membership is useful in labour negotiations.

It is fairly common practice to include with the strength breakdown a return of the numbers of new starters, leavers and transfers, indicating sex, skill, department, etc. This can be represented in both numbers and percentages of total intake or leavers as follows:

	Number	Percentage
Under 26		
26–30		
31–35		
36–40		
41–45		
46–50		
Over 50		

The total departmental figures for the previous year may be shown on the sheet, for one of the main uses of the return is to highlight changes. A third coloumn may be used to show the difference in the figures. In many firms, however, management prefer to compare the whole sheet with the corresponding return for a year or more back. The return, though maintained on a week-to-week basis, is usually circulated to managers monthly, but where a firm is reasonably stable, a quarterly return may suffice.

Sources of data

There are three methods for collecting figures for the strength of returns. One source is the day journal, mentioned in Chapter 4, though it is advisable to make a complete count from basic records periodically as a cross-check.

The second approach is to make a count from employee history sheets or from the visible index records and thus construct both a strength breakdown and a wide range of statistical tables, such as an age breakdown, a service breakdown and an analysis of direct and indirect workers according to department. Such a periodic count is only possible and useful in very small firms. If, however, visible index cards (Figure 3:10) are used a statistical card at the end of each tray is a simple way of keeping up to date. The gross totals can then be computed by adding the departmental totals.

The third method is the use of statistical cards which may be complementary to other systems, and in which relevant data is arranged in such a way as to facilitate counting.

Figure 3:1   Notification of employee engagement form
Copies are printed on coloured paper to simplify routing procedures

```
┌─────────────────────────────────────────────────────────────────────┐
│               NOTIFICATION OF EMPLOYEE ENGAGEMENT                     │
├─────────────────────────────────────────────────────────────────────┤
│                                                                       │
│    Surname _____        Married/single      │
│                                                                       │
│    Forenames _____                            │
│                                                                       │
│    Address _____                            │
│                                                                       │
│            _____                            │
│                                                                       │
│    Date of commencement _____                                 │
│                                                                       │
│    Dates if previously employed _____                            │
│                                                                       │
│    Born _____         Age _____                    │
│                                                                       │
│    Dept _____         Clock No _____               │
│                                                                       │
│    Job _____         Hours _____                  │
│                                                                       │
│    Rate of pay _____                                          │
│                                                                       │
│  Signature _____        Routing – WHITE COPY – Cashier      │
│                                          PINK COPY   – Floor Manager  │
│                  Personnel dept          BLUE COPY  – Employment Office│
│                                                                       │
└─────────────────────────────────────────────────────────────────────┘
```

Figure 3:2 New staff employee form

This is a four-copy set: one copy goes to the personnel department, one to the wages department, one is for internal use and one is for filing (George Cohen 600 Group Limited)

From _____		
To Group Personnel Department		
Full names		Company/location
Address		Telephone number
Job title		Salary
Date of start	Date of birth	Banker
Hours of work	Marital status	National Insurance number
Other details		Signed _____ Date _____

Figure 3:3 Certificate P45

This is Part 3 of the Inland Revenue form which is handed over to the departing employee along with Part 2. Both parts are given to the new employer who must then complete Part 3 and send it immediately to the local tax office. See also Figure 8:4

INCOME TAX : NEW EMPLOYEE
PART 3
PARTICULARS OF OLD EMPLOYMENT

1. Old employer's PAYE reference

2. Employee's National Insurance number

3. Employee's surname
   Mr. Mrs. Miss etc.
   Employee's first two forenames

4. Date of leaving — Day | Month | Year

5. Code at date of leaving "X" indicates Week 1 (Month 1) basis — Code | Wk. 1 (or Month 1)

6. Last entries on Deduction Card (except where "X" is entered at item 5)
   Week or Month No. — Week | Month
   Total pay to date £
   Total tax to date £ p

NEW EMPLOYER–Please complete items 7 to 14 and send this form to your Tax Office IMMEDIATELY. Please also read the instructions on Part 2.

7. New employer's PAYE reference

8. Date employment commenced (Enter in figures) — Day | Month | Year 19

9. Enter "✓" if you require these items to be shown on Deduction Cards, etc. "✓"
   Works No.
   Branch, Dept.

10. Enter "P" if this employee will not be paid by you between date shown at item 8 and the next 5 April — P | FOR CENTRE USE | N/D | P47 | M/E | DOM | HP

11. If tax entered at item 6 does not agree tax entered on Deduction Card from the Tax Tables, state here the Tax Table figure. £

12. Employee's private address

13. Nature of employment

14. DECLARATION
    I have prepared a Deduction Card in accordance with the above particulars.
    FOR CENTRE USE | Ind Cd | T

    Employer

    Address

    Date

P45

Figure 3:4　Certificate P46

This form is to be completed for a new employee for whom no code number has been notified to the employer. The employer must then prepare a deduction card and deduct tax using the Emergency Code Table (P15)

Income tax
EMPLOYEE FOR WHOM NO CODE NOTIFIED TO EMPLOYER

This form should be completed only where, for an employee, in any class below, the form P8 (BLUE CARD) instructs you to send form P46 to your Tax Office. It should not be sent in any other circumstances.

Instructions on the completion of Deduction Cards and the use of Tax Tables are given on form P8 (BLUE CARD).

1. Employer's PAYE reference number ....

2. Employee's National Insurance number

3. Employee's Surname
   (in BLOCK letters)　　.. Mr/Mrs/Miss

   Christian or other forenames　..

4. Employee's private address　..

   ....

5. CLASS OF EMPLOYEE
   Enter "√" in the box which applies to employee
   Rate of pay exceeds taxable limits shown on P8(BLUE CARD)

   NEW EMPLOYEE　{　　1. School leaver　　　　　　　　　　　1 ☐

   　　　　　　　　　　2. Other employee with no P45　　　2 ☐

   EXISTING EMPLOYEE　{　3. In your employment at 6 April but no Deduction Card received　　3 ☐

   　　　　　　　　　　4. Previously paid below the taxable limit　　4 ☐

   Rate of pay exceeds £1 but does not exceed limit shown on P8(BLUE CARD)
   ANY EMPLOYEE　　5. With other employment　　5 ☐

6. Date employment commenced if after 5 April last *(enter in figures)*　| Day | Month | Year |

7. Works No. ....　Branch Dept. etc.　..

8. If heading 5 of item 5 applies enter average weekly rate of pay　£

9. If employee is a woman, state if known, whether married, widow, single, etc.

10. Nature of employment

Employer ....
(Use BLOCK letters)
Address　..

....　Date........................ 197.....

PLEASE DO NOT WRITE IN THIS SPACE

P46　　　　　　　　　　　　　　　　　　MP 212468 1/76 52-9284

Figure 3:5   Engagement induction checklist

This indicates when information should be given. Two ticks against an item signify a brief outline prior to employment with a more detailed explanation later

CHECKLIST I	Pre-employment	First day	After 10 days and before 8 weeks	Informal follow-up
(A) Employment conditions				
Remuneration	✓			
Method of payment (how, when, where)		✓		
Make-up of pay (bonus, merit rating and other plus rates)	✓			✓
Hours of work	✓			
Overtime–availability and arrangement	✓		✓	
Holidays			✓	
Sickness payment scheme			✓	
Pension scheme	✓		✓	
Profit sharing or irregular bonus			✓	
Notice period			✓	
(B) Procedures				
Explanation of wage and salary slip				✓
Time recording and keeping		✓		
Absence			✓	
Certification requirements			✓	
(C) Health, safety, and welfare				
Medical examination	✓			
Medical centres, surgery		✓		
First aid regulations		✓		
Dental and other medical facilities			✓	
Safety (regulations, appliances)		✓		
Protective clothing		✓	✓	
Fire precaution procedures		✓	✓	
Smoking		✓		
Canteen facilities		✓		
Sports and social club			✓	
Recreation facilities			✓	
(D) General				
Joint consultation (works advisory committee, works council, etc)			✓	
Grievance procedure			✓	
Trade union membership	✓		✓	
Education and training			✓	
Department organisation			✓	
Individual and departmental work targets			✓	
Promotion and transfers			✓	✓
Security arrangements		✓		
Personal problems				✓
Purchase facilities			✓	
Saving schemes			✓	
Suggestion scheme			✓	
Car and bicycle parking facilities	✓			

Figure 3:6   Engagement checklist
Provides a list of action to be taken from when an offer letter is sent until the new employee is included on all necessary forms and lists (Greater London Council)

Greater London Council
Department of Public Health Engineering
Appointment/Engagement – face sheet

Name: _____   Grade: _____
DOE: _____   Loc/Div: _____
Salary: _____   N.I. No. _____

	Date	Remarks
1) Offer sent		
2) Offer accepted		
(a) References		
(b) Medical		
(c) Notifications		
(d) Birth Cert. checked		
3) Action after commencement		
(a) (i) P.100 to TR		
(ii) Bank Form		
(iii) P.45		
(iv) CSF 64		
(v) M.M.A.		
(vi) P60 Details		
(viii) Allowances		
(b) Noted in Starter's book		
(c) Probationary Report Book		
(d) Index card/overtime card		
(e) Leave card		
(f) Chargeability code		
(g) TR/SUP/1		
(a) Received		
(b) To TR/D1		
(h) Staff list		
(i) Salary list		
(j) Safety booklet issued		

Figure 3:7   Employer's application for authority to refund tax to new employee (P47)

See instructions overleaf

Income tax

Employer's application for authority to refund tax to new employee

1. Name of employee ....

2. National Insurance number

3. Works No./Branch,
   Dept., Contract, etc. ....

4. Employer's PAYE reference number ....

A refund exceeding £50 is due to the above named employee on his first pay day with me. Please authorise me to make this refund.

Employer   ....

Address   ....
*(Including
postcode
if any)*   ....

              ....

Date ....197.........

For official use

P48 issued ....

P47

212905 52–9849 McC

Figure 3:7 *continued*

Instructions

Refund to new employee

If the Tables show that a refund exceeding £50 is due to a new employee on his first pay day-

    (a) enter in column 7 of the Deduction Card the amount repayable; mark the entry "RN" but do not make the refund,

    (b) complete this form (P47) and send it to the Tax Office at once,

    (c) make the refund on receipt of the authority from the Tax Office on form P48.

Tax deductions on the second and subsequent pay days should proceed as though the refund had actually been made, and any refund which may become due on **those pay days** should be made whether or not the authority from the Tax Office to make the refund due on the first pay day has been received.

Figure 3:8　Statement of terms and conditions of employment

THIS STATEMENT SETS OUT CERTAIN PARTICULARS OF THE TERMS AND CONDITIONS ON WHICH YOU ARE EMPLOYED.

Name and Address of Employer	Name and Address of Employee	Male	Single
		Female	Married
			Widowed
		Date of birth	

Occupation (State Job Title)	Department	Check No.	Date emp'ment comm'ced

* Your employment with your previous employer does not count as part of your continuous period of employment.

* Your previous employment with_____

counts as part of your continuous period of employment which therefore began on_____

　*DELETE AS APPROPRIATE

PENSIONS:
　(a) The Employer does not operate a Staff Pension Scheme
　(b) The Employer operates a Contributory/Non Contributory Pension Scheme and full details are available from:—

National Insurance No.

NORMAL HOURS OF WORK (Include details of rest periods, meal breaks etc.)

OVERTIME
　(a) Carries no extra remuneration
　(b) Carries extra remuneration as follows:—

REMUNERATION
is at the rate of £_____ per_____
and is paid at_____ intervals
and will normally be paid on_____
for earnings up to_____

PAID HOLIDAYS each year

(a) Statutory or Public Holidays_____days per year payable at the_____rate of pay in respect of

(b) Annual Holidays
　(i) In accordance with the National Agreement relating to the_____industry. Entitlement is
　(ii) On the following basis

If employment is terminated before the holidays have been taken accrued holiday pay will be added to the final payment in respect of the completed period of notice in accordance with the following regulations:—

SICKNESS or INJURY.

In the event of incapacity for work due to sickness or injury the following action should be taken.

(a) No payment will be made for time lost.
(b) Payment will be made on receipt of a medical certificate within the first_____days of incapacity on the following scale.

TERMINATION OF EMPLOYMENT — STATUTORY MINIMUM
(a) EMPLOYEE:—After 4 weeks' service — 1 week's notice will be required.
(b) EMPLOYER:—After 4 weeks' service — 1 week's notice will be given.
　　　　After 2 years' service — 1 week's notice for each complete year of service up to a maximum of 12 weeks.

If contract is for a fixed term delete periods of notice and state expiry date_____

ADDITIONS TO STATUTORY MINIMUM, IF ANY:—

DISCIPLINARY RULES (Give particulars and/or state where rules may be consulted)

If dissatisfied with any disciplinary decision relating to you, you should refer the matter verbally or in writing to:—

GRIEVANCE PROCEDURE: If you have a grievance it should be referred verbally or in writing to_____
If no immediate settlement the procedure set out in
_____will be followed.
Further information in respect of the terms of employment may be obtained on application to:—
Any changes in the terms of employment will be notified as they occur.

A contracting-out certificate under the Social Security Pensions Act 1975 is/is not in force in respect of employment to which this statement refers.

Employee's signature confirming receipt of statement
　　　　　　　Date

Figure 3:9   Basic personnel file

Individual card strips with basic information are used to form a basic register of
employees. The card strips can be easily moved for inserting and withdrawing
(Kalamazoo Limited)

Surname		Christian names			Married	Clock No
Address		Date of birth	Grade		Single	
					Nat Ins No	
		Date commenced	Dept		Former employer	
		Date terminated	Rate	S B	H P	
463157						

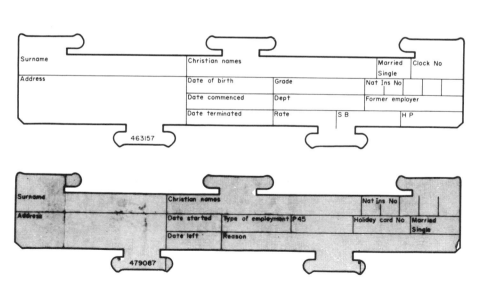

Surname		Christian names			Nat Ins No	
Address		Date started	Type of employment	P45	Holiday card No	Married
		Date left	Reason			Single
479067						

Figure 3:10   Visible-edge personnel index

Larger record cards are filed to overlap one another so that only the edges containing the employees' names are shown (Kardex Systems (UK) Ltd)

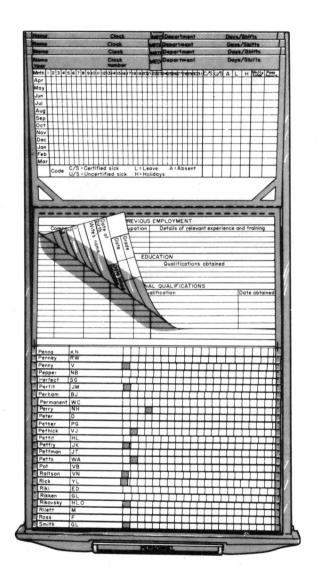

4

Personal History Records

The basic essential in every personnel department is a record of the personal history of every employee while he is with the firm, with such other background material as will assist in giving a comprehensive picture of him as an employee.

In some systems the application form is used as the personal history form. Little of the information need then be transferred to other documents. The layout of the application form must be specifically designed to fulfil this function and placed in a readily accessible position in the employee's file. In most firms, however, a separate personal history card is maintained.

Once again, one must decide just what information should be included on the personal record form. Every piece of information should be considered on its merit and unless it serves a purpose it should be eliminated. There are many personal history records which contain information of questionable value – for example, the names of the employee's children, relatives working for the firm, his personal doctor or his religion. This sort of data creates a lot of additional work that cannot be justified by its value. At the same time, other much more relevant data may be left out.

Below are suggested items of information which could be considered essential:

Surname	Forename	Identification number
Business address		
Residence		
Home telephone		
Name of spouse	Number of children	
Date of birth	Place of birth	
Date commenced employment		
Contact in emergency:	Name	
	Address	
	Place of employment	
	Relationship	

Information might also be needed on race, sex and marital status, but such details should be used with care.

Medical restrictions   Physical disabled register
Physical examinations
Employee grade or group
Union code
In-company location code
Department, group section
Payroll number   Tax code
Major accidents
Bank/Giro account number
Parking lot number
Gate pass number
Job classification code
Termination   Type   Date
Retirement   Date
Security clearance

Non-essential information which may nevertheless be useful could include:

Professional associations
Examinations completed
Educational achievements
Languages   Proficiency
Military service
Military training
Skills   Type   Experience
Management experience
Test scores
Union membership
Previous employment

Some firms continue the practice of pasting a photograph of the employee on his record card, though there would seem to be little reason for doing so. Photographs are useful for trainee records so that former instructors and supervisors can recognise them more easily in later years when passing judgement. Some firms need photographs for security purposes. Companies with staff extended throughout the country, such as multiple retail stores, or with overseas interests, find it useful to have photographs as head officials often wish to see them before they are about to visit their offices.

Personal history cards can be used to keep a record of the employee's work performance, achievement both in his work and socially, accidents, absences and details of any disciplinary action.

Design and Format

Ideally, the personal history form should complement the application form or any other forms from which the information is obtained in the first place, in order to minimise errors in transferring data. At the same time the most significant and most frequently used information should be at the top or side of the form on which it can be easily seen without withdrawing the whole card from the file.

It is helpful to design the record card so that all permanent information is separated from the other items which are likely to change, such as addresses. Ford Motor Company in the US separates information obtained from applicants, additional information gathered while employed and information on former employees acquired after termination.

In some firms information subject to change is written on the record in pencil or adhesive labels which can be removed. A record of changes in status, education or wage rates may be a relevant part of the employee's history, however; it is better to allow sufficient space for the amendment of such items with a new line stating the up-to-date position every time there is a change in any one particular. This gives the current positions and the history at a glance. In those industries where wages are related to the cost of living index, a separate wage notebook is usually kept, as it would be impossible to amend all the cards for every minor change.

Types of Record Cards

In general a card is kept for every employee in a separate file. Figures 4:1 and 4:2 show examples of personal history records which should be printed on thick paper for individual filing. In some instances, the records of trainees are kept separately, but the division of the file into too many sections may lead to confusion and wasted time searching. It is by far better to flag individual cards filed in straight alphabetical order, to indicate whether they are trainees, worthy of promotion, etc.

A number of firms prefer to keep all records and correspondence regarding an individual together. The personal history form can be printed on a manila folder or envelope which can be used to contain all other documents. Figure 4:3 shows an example of a combined personal history card and correspondence container. Figure 4:4 illustrates an envelope-type file cover. This method has a disadvantage in that details have to be recorded by hand and all the papers stored inside must be taken out before additional information can be recorded or amendments made. On the other hand, information on each employee is more easily available, and it is less easy to lose small documents.

Visible-edge records

With a visible-edge filing system, the forms are designed so that the pertinent information is inserted on the edge of the form for easier reference. The forms are arranged so that they overlap one another to form an index. (See Figure 3:10.)

There are several different makes of visible-index forms specifically designed for use in personnel records but manufacturers will design forms to meet the particular needs of companies.

Visible-edge forms can be kept in a flat tray or a loose-leaf binder. Figure 4:5 shows an example of a personal history card designed for a drawer tray. Figures 4:6 and 4:7 illustrate personnel forms for filing in a loose-leaf binder. These are usually printed on normal paper stock. Forms designed for filing in flat trays are usually printed on heavier stock and entries normally have to be made by hand. They are secured at the top edge and insertions and withdrawals can be slow and time-consuming. On the other hand, ring binders tend to be large and bulky. Trays of cards are in mobile segments and can be detached for putting on a desk. Alternatively, the whole unit can be stored in a trolley for moving it easily about the office.

Retrieval Systems

Virtually every piece of information held on an individual card can be coded for identification and retrieval. It is possible, for example, to indicate by codes the time when a particular record requires action. This is particularly important in large firms where an individual could easily be ignored for long periods, unless he himself took the initiative.

Records of employees who are scheduled to receive an increase in their basic rate on their eighteenth or twenty-first birthday should be coded according to month and year of birth. The system could also be designed to throw up a record of an employee when he becomes eligible for a staff insurance or other benefits, or when he is due to have his salary reviewed.

In the same way a system can be devised to identify experience and skills of employees. Such systems need not be sophisticated, once the characteristics are coded. In this way it is possible to select those most suitable for training courses, when the opportunity arises, and identify those worthy of promotion.

By coding personal records by age, regular lists of key and senior personnel scheduled to retire can be obtained. In times of redundancy it is possible to select men over sixty-five and women over sixty and those nearing retirement, to minimise the effect of redundancy on the whole labour force.

Similarly, records can be coded according to date of engagement to indicate length of service so that, in times of redundancy, the personnel department is able to identify those most recently recruited. Another code can be used to denote records of those possessing skills which are considered indispensable to the firm.

It is also useful to identify employees trained in first-aid treatment. According to the First-Aid (Standard of Training) Order 1960, no one can be deemed to be trained in first-aid treatment unless he or she is a registered or enrolled assistant nurse, or a holder of a certificate in first aid issued by a training organisation within the previous three years, or is otherwise recognised as being qualified in first-aid treatment by a training organisation, such as the St John Ambulance Association.

Coding methods

Records can be most easily coded with labels or tabs of different colours or shapes to denote various characteristics or attributes. It is easy, of course, for a coding system to become too sophisticated, so that the whole set-up becomes unwieldly. It is up to the personnel manager to ensure that any coding system does not become so complicated that the codes stop having any significance to the clerks using it.

If visible-edge cards are used, key characteristics such as age group, professional qualifications, date of engagement, etc, can be indicated on the leading edge and identified, when required, with different coloured tabs in cellulose or acetate strips provided to protect the cards from wear and tear. Figures 4:8 to 4:10 show examples of visible-edge records designed to be coded for identification and retrieval.

Hand-operated sorting systems

Forms printed on heavy stock may be coded by holes punched in the body or the edge of the card and selected by means of spindles or rods. There are many such forms on the market designed specifically for the personnel function. Basically there are three types – slotted, notched and edge-punched cards. In all three types, holes are punched in predetermined spaces to designate the particular characteristics by which the cards may be sorted. In this way, it is possible to select cards with one or several characteristics in common.

In the first type, the holes are slotted in the body of the card. The features are represented by positions between two holes. The holes are then connected to form slots about 10 mm long, if the items recorded on the card possess the features represented by the positions. The advantage of this type over the others is that the slot allows the cards to fall, but they cannot fall right out of the pack and do not have to be replaced. They remain in their proper place.

The cards are placed in a cradle, the spindles are inserted as required and the cradle is then inverted so that the cards fall upside down. When the cradle is brought back to its normal position, the selected cards are upstanding and the name or other pertinent information is visible from the top of the rest of the pack.

Figures 4:11 and 4:12 show examples of body-punched history cards. Figure 4:12, in addition to the personal details which are recorded on the top of the card, provides the following classifications in the selecting field:

1 *Year of birth* Positions 1 to 11 are used in a two-rod combination code to cover the years 1891 to 1945 inclusive
2 *Month of birth* Positions 12 to 17 are used in the same way to give the months January to December

3	*Year of joining*	Positions 21 to 31 cover the years 1908 to 1962
4	*Month of joining*	Positions 32 to 37 again cover the 12 months
5	*Educational*	Positions 51 to 65 are allotted singly to educational qualifications including stage of apprenticeship
6	*Seniority*	Positions 71 to 80 are allotted singly to seniority level based on five-yearly periods
9	*Status*	Positions 84 to 90 are allotted singly to staff grouping

In this example, additional single positions are allotted to such items as day, night or piece worker, married or single, medical category, etc. Numbers 38, 39 and 40 are left as spares for additional headings, and various other sections have spare positions to allow for expansion.

In the second type, the features on the edge of the card are clipped. A rod is inserted in a jogger which vibrates the cards, causing those with desired characteristics to fall into place. Only those cards notched where the rod is situated will fall. If several rods are inserted in the jogger, only those cards notched in every position corresponding to a rod will fall. In this way it is possible to isolate cards with several characteristics in common.

The third type are purchased with a series of pre-punched holes on their edge. The holes, with the desired features, are slotted. A spindle is then inserted through the pack, in the desired hole, and lifted, isolating the cards with the perforations. The process is repeated with the remaining cards should a further division be required.

Figures 4:13 to 4:16 show examples of edge-punched history cards.

Notices of Change

It is essential, of course, that the personnel department is advised of any changes in the employee's status so that the information on his personal record may be kept up to date. There are several ways for the personnel department to keep itself informed of changes in an employee's status. Blank cards shaped like a clock card are sometimes made available at employee's entrances. The employee records changes and leaves it with the clock card or, if he prefers, hands it to the personnel department or his supervisor. Data can also be gathered from routine documents processed on a regular basis.

Many firms send a questionnaire to all employees annually. A more complete return is obtained, incidentally, if this is done through the supervisor rather than through the post or pay envelopes. Staff may be asked for changes at the time of the annual salary review or performance appraisal.

Amendment forms

In some companies a separate form is used to report each type of change, and in some instances even initiate the change. Figure 4:17, for example, shows a notification of transfer or other change of status. In other firms a single form is designed to serve all changes possible during an employee's service, with the exception of terminations and employee requisitions. Examples of composite forms designed for a variety of purposes are shown in Figures 4:18 and 4:19.

Usually the contents of an amendment form contain the nature of the change, the name and clock number of the employee concerned, the effective date of the change and, in the case of a transfer, the new clock number which is inserted by the personnel department before the form is routed.

In some cases only one copy of the form is issued and is circulated to all departments concerned. It is normally initiated by the supervisor, sent to the line manager for authorisation if necessary and passed on to the personnel department to be recorded before it is distributed. In other firms several copies are raised and sent directly to the appropriate departments including Personnel.

Where there are many changes each week, duplicated lists are prepared to notify every department, even though individual change notes may have been raised and passed to the personnel department for action. This information could also be included among other items in the employees' magazine or newsletter.

In some firms the training and management development functions are provided not only with changes but also with impending changes and promotions, anticipated changes in the managerial structure and new positions being created. This is to assist the training staff to plan their training schedules and determine training needs in advance.

The Journal

Many personnel departments maintain a 'day book' or journal in which are recorded new entrants, terminations, transfers, changed rates, etc. This is to provide a daily record of all employee movements and to be used in preparing other records and statistics. It is particularly useful if only the minimum of forms are used.

Such a journal also has value as a history or reference book. It can be used in follow-up procedures as it is easy to pick out those employees who joined the company a month, three months, or a year ago, and it can give a very quick picture of trends in labour turnover.

The details to be recorded will depend on the information needed. The 'new starters' section could include columns covering:

1 Actual date of starting
2 Reference or clock number
3 Name and sex
4 Age
5 Address

6   Job
7   Basic rate

Terminations could have columns detailing:

1   Personal factors
2   Reason for termination (divided into controllable and uncontrollable)
3   Length of service

Changes in particulars include all changes in the employee's status, such as rate and job.

An example of a journal divided into sections is shown in Figure 4:20.

Figure 4:1   Personal history record

Name			Date of joining	
Nationality	Remuneration		Date of leaving	
	Date	Amount	Reason	
Date of birth				
Marital status				
Number of children at time of joining			Region/division	
Qualifications			Permanent transfers	
			Date	Region
Languages (fluent)				
			Promotions	
			Date	Position
			•	

Experience prior to joining ABC Limited			
Date		Position	Company
From	To		

Periods of illness (over 2 weeks)		
Date		Nature of illness
From	To	

Figure 4:2 Personal history record

Name								
Address					Date of birth			
					Married or single			
					Children			
Education					Date commenced			
					A or *B* list			
Degrees: exams					Tests			
Qualifications								
Previous employers								

Date	Amount of increase	Current salary	Remarks	Date	Amount of increase	Current salary	Remarks

			History					
Date	Division	Department	Job title	Date	Division	Department	Job title	Special gifts

Date	General remarks

Figure 4:3 Combined personal history card and correspondence container
Certain information is recorded on this cover, though a further history card is placed inside the pocket together with other relevant papers concerning the employee

Date of Birth			Pension Fund Date		
Occupation	L'ATE				
	FROM	TO	Group Insurance: Date		Class
			Date Asbestos Exam		
			Date X Ray		
			R D P No	C L	Fumes
			Heavy Work	Ears	Asbestos
			Outside Work	Eyes	Resins
			Date passed	Dr	
			Remarks		
Age Group	Name	No	Dept		Asb Reg

Figure 4:4 Envelope-type personal file cover
The envelope is used to record personal details and history. The reverse side has space for a brief résumé of the education and training record, a note of company activities the employee engages in and a section for general remarks

Surname _____ Forenames _____ M/S/W_____ Works No_____
Address _____
1st change of address _____
2nd change of address _____
Date of birth _____ Nat Ins No / / / / Trade union _____
Registered as disabled_____RDP No _____ Date of expiry_____
Next of kin (name, address, tel No) _____

Date engaged	Date left	Total service	Reason for termination	
				Reserve liability _____
				Date of entry into W P F _____
				Whether to be re-employed _____
				National date for coy service _____ assessment

OCCUPATIONAL CHANGES

Date	Dept	Shift	Occupation	Rate	Reason for change	Date	Dept	Shift	Occupation	Rate	Reason for change

Figure 4:5   Personal history record, drawer tray visible edge

The reverse side has columns for rates of pay, space for special interview notes and reason for leaving. It is designed to fold in half

Date	Department	Previous employment	Reasons for transfer

PREVIOUS EMPLOYMENT			
Name of firm	Years	Capacity	Reason left

Surname Nat Ins No	Medical examination Date started
Christian names	Engaged as Dept
Address	Rate on engagement Clock No
	Panel Doctor

Reg D P

Date of birth	Place of birth (Nat)	Single	Married	Widow(er)	National service record		
					Period		Conduct
	No of children				Force		Rank or job
					War disability		

Next of kin		Relative in company's employ		
Name Relationship		Name	Relationship	Position
Address				

Education				
Name of school	Grade	Standard	Period	
				Company handbooks issued
Later education – special qualifications – exams passed				

I have received the company's handbooks mentioned above and have read them

Signature   Date

Surname	Christian names	Clock No	Dept	Follow ups & wage increase due											
				Jan	Feb	Mar	Apr	May	Jun	Jul	Aug	Sep	Oct	Nov	Dec

Figure 4:6　Personal history record

This is an example of a visible-edge record sheet for inserting in a loose-leaf binder

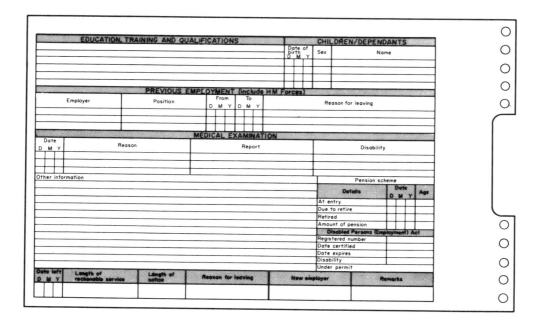

Figure 4:7 Staff record card

This form is similar to the one shown in Figure 4:6 but is designed for recording information on staff

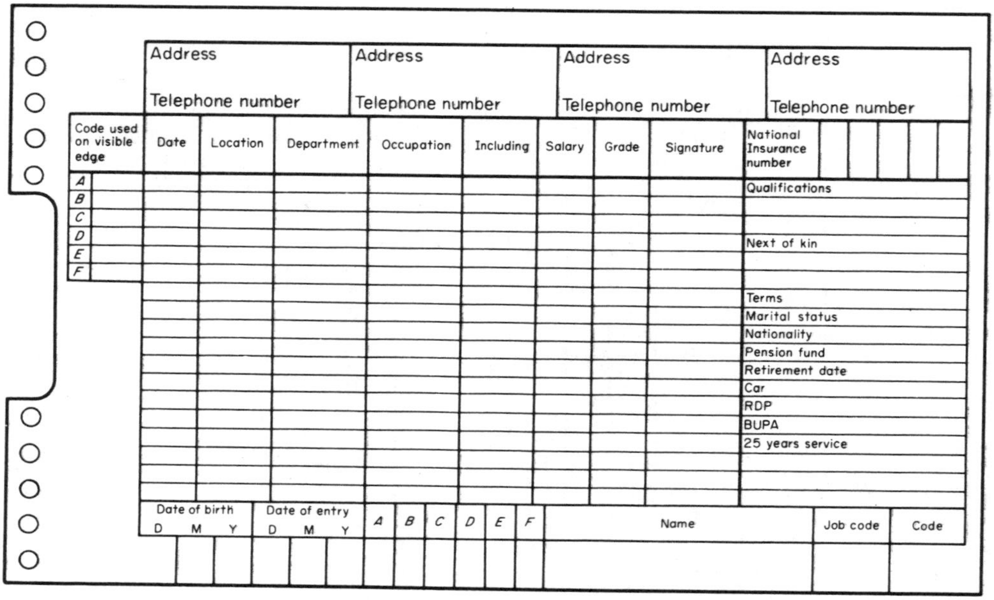

Address | Address | Address | Address

Telephone number | Telephone number | Telephone number | Telephone number

Code used on visible edge	Date	Location	Department	Occupation	Including	Salary	Grade	Signature	National Insurance number
A									Qualifications
B									
C									
D									Next of kin
E									
F									
									Terms
									Marital status
									Nationality
									Pension fund
									Retirement date
									Car
									RDP
									BUPA
									25 years service

Date of birth D M Y	Date of entry D M Y	A	B	C	D	E	F	Name	Job code	Code

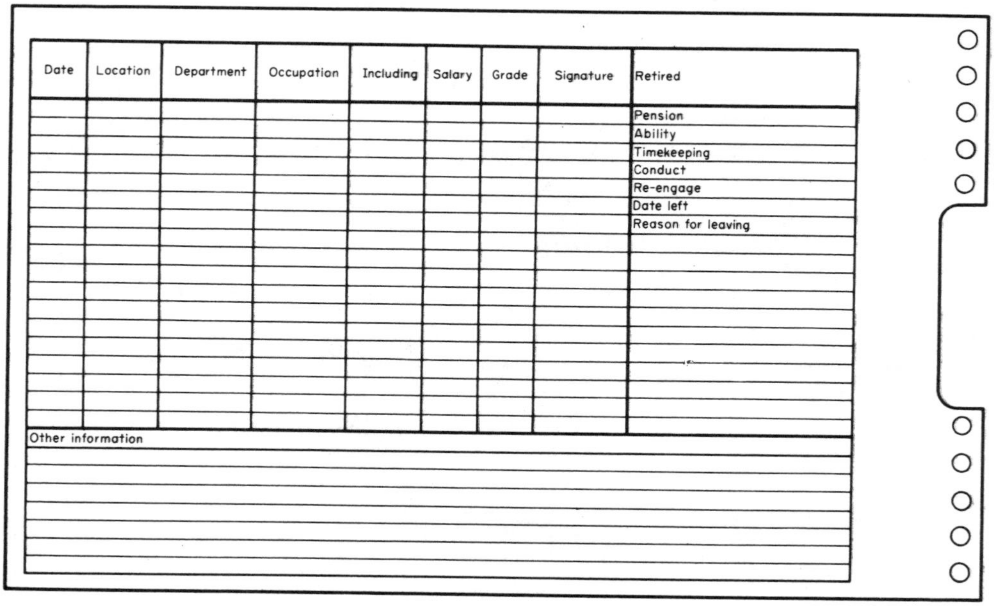

Date	Location	Department	Occupation	Including	Salary	Grade	Signature	Retired
								Pension
								Ability
								Timekeeping
								Conduct
								Re-engage
								Date left
								Reason for leaving

Other information

Figure 4:8 Coded personal history record

This is an example of a simple single-card personal record designed by Kardex Systems (UK) Ltd. A signal over the appropriate age group gives the employee's age, but it would be better, if space were available, to indicate date of birth since this would not require annual up-dating. The employee's trade classification is signalled to indicate that he is skilled, semi-skilled or a trainee. If the employee is engaged part-time only, a signal is placed over the space headed PT.

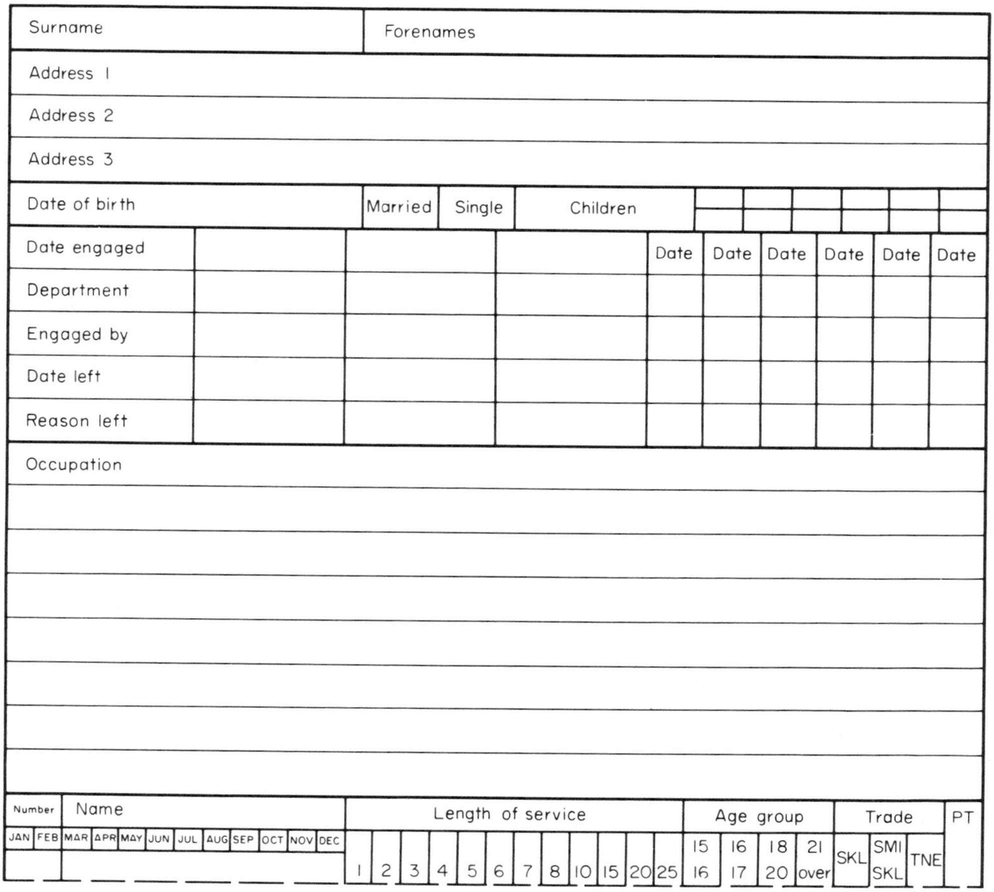

Surname		Forenames									
Address 1											
Address 2											
Address 3											
Date of birth		Married	Single	Children							
Date engaged						Date	Date	Date	Date	Date	Date
Department											
Engaged by											
Date left											
Reason left											
Occupation											

Number	Name	Length of service		Age group				Trade			PT
JAN FEB MAR APR MAY JUN JUL AUG SEP OCT NOV DEC		1 2 3 4 5 6 7 8 10 15 20 25		15 16	16 17	18 20	21 over	SKL	SMI SKL	TNE	

Figure 4:9   Coded personal history record
This form is folded into two parts, with the basic information immediately visible and
other information inside. The 1 to 26 scale is used to denote the next salary review.
Different coloured signals are used for each half year. The coding 1 to 8 denotes
which department or section of the business the employee is engaged in. For
example, number 4 could represent the drawing office (Kardex Systems (UK) Ltd)

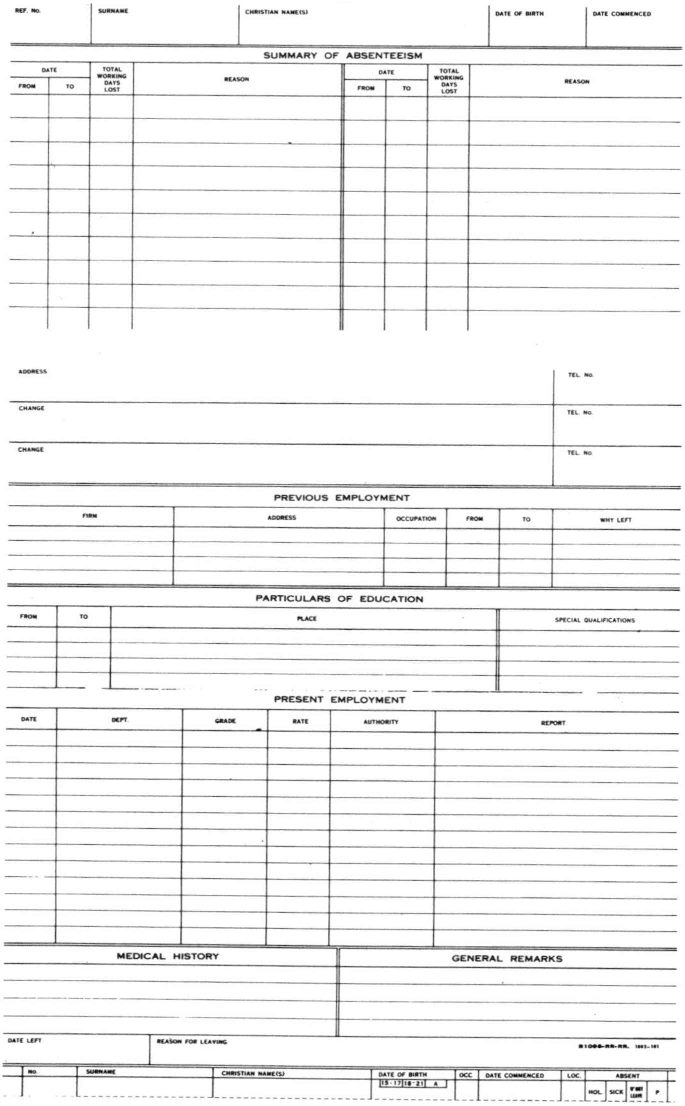

Figure 4:10 Coded personal history record

This card was designed to customer specification. The visible edge is fixed so that the folder form can be replaced easily. Its removal is signified by the round-punched hole in the title insert. The 1 to 52 scale denotes, by means of a coloured signal, the next salary review. The signalling on the far right denotes commitments other than those of work. In this company, two colours are used for the title insert – blue for male employees and pink for females (Kardex Systems (UK) Ltd)

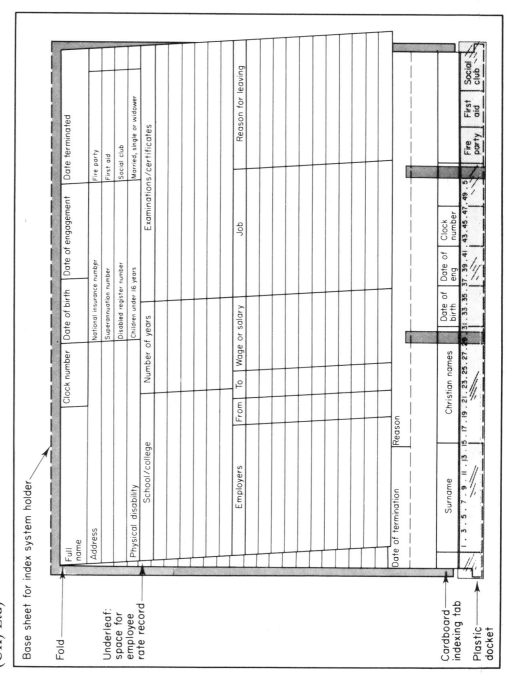

Figure 4:11 Body-punched personal history card
Slots are cut in certain areas to show particular characteristics of the employee, such as age, marital status and education. The card has two sections, the 'recording field' for written or typed information and the 'selecting field' for statistical information (C. W. Cave)

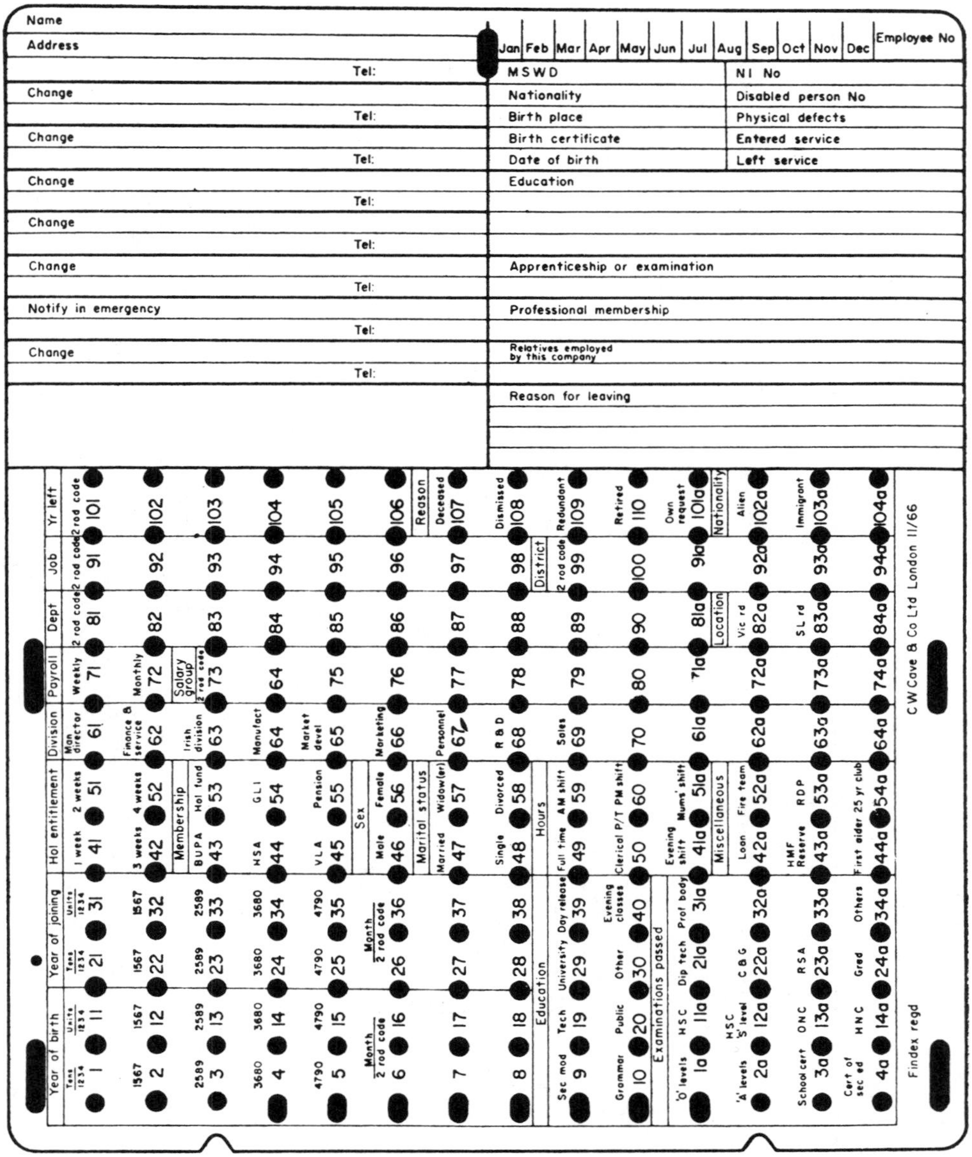

Figure 4:12   Body-punched history card

In this example, the card has been slotted for a male (47) group leader (87) born in 1925 (slot 3 and 6) with a secondary school education (51). He is married (41), in medical category *A* (68) and joined the firm in 1954 (24 and 31). An amendment has been made in area 92 (C.W. Cave)

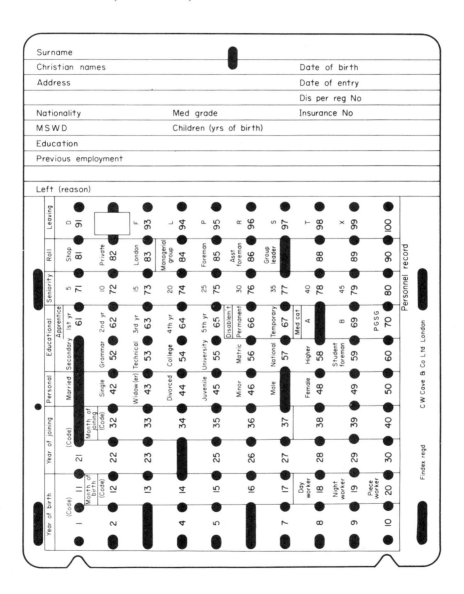

Figure 4:13   Edge-punched personal history card (Copeland-Chatterson)

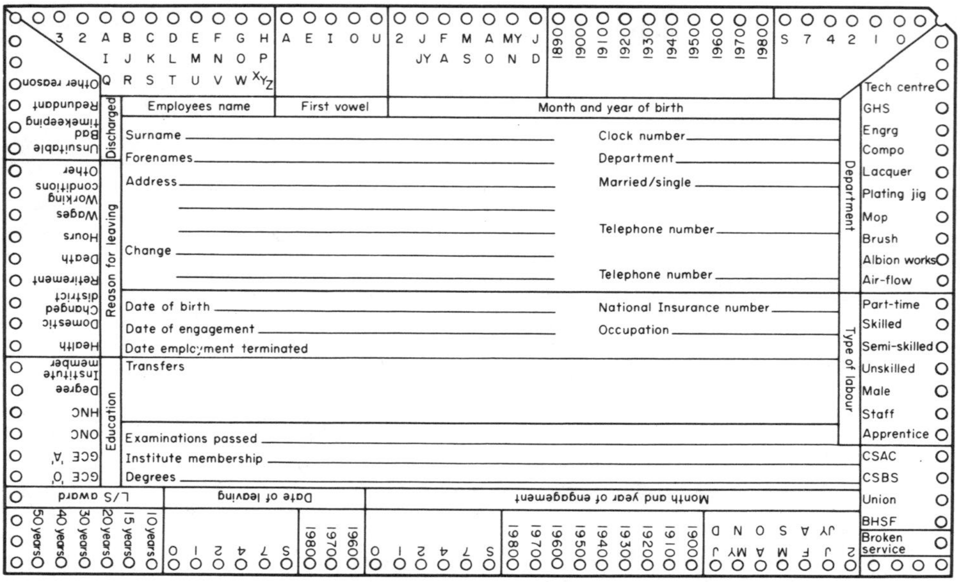

Figure 4:14   Edge-punched personal history card (Copeland-Chatterson)

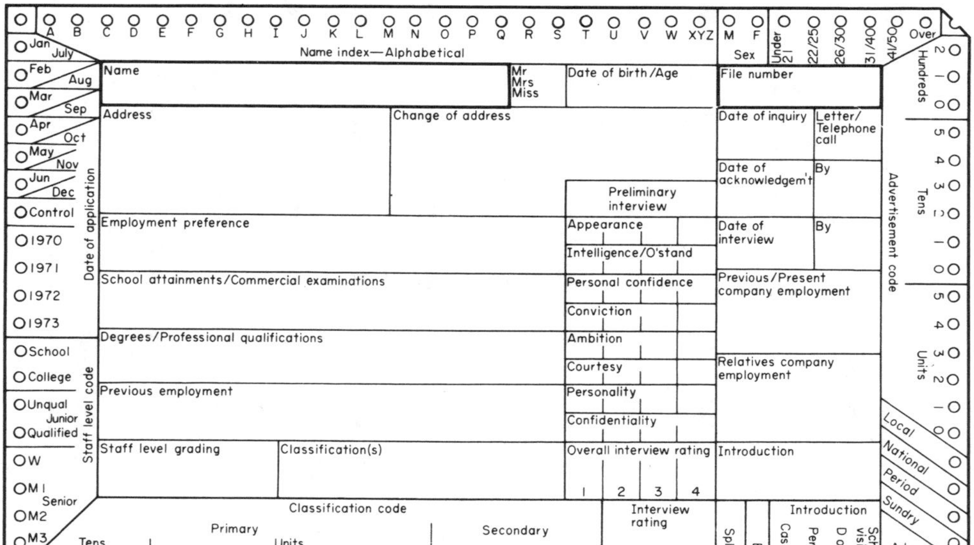

Figure 4:15 Edge-punched personal history card (Copeland-Chatterson)

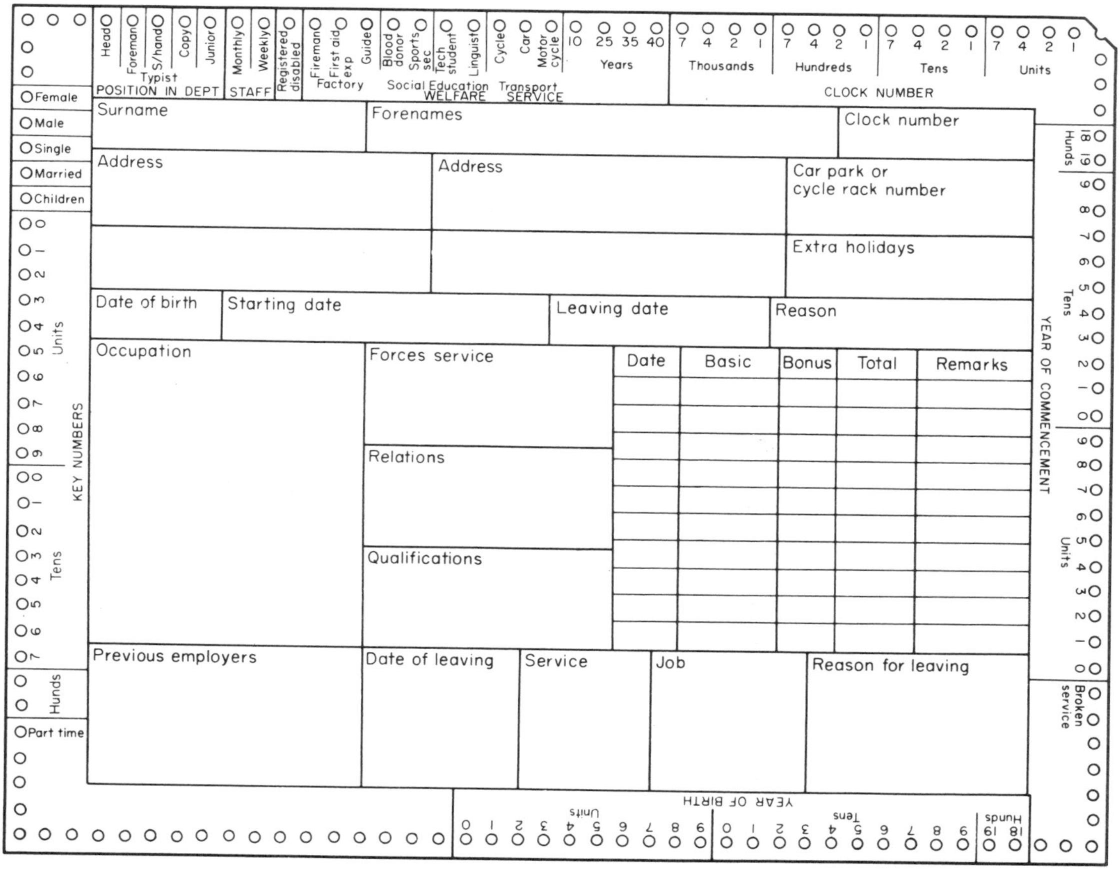

Figure 4:16 Edge-punched personal history card (Copeland-Chatterson)

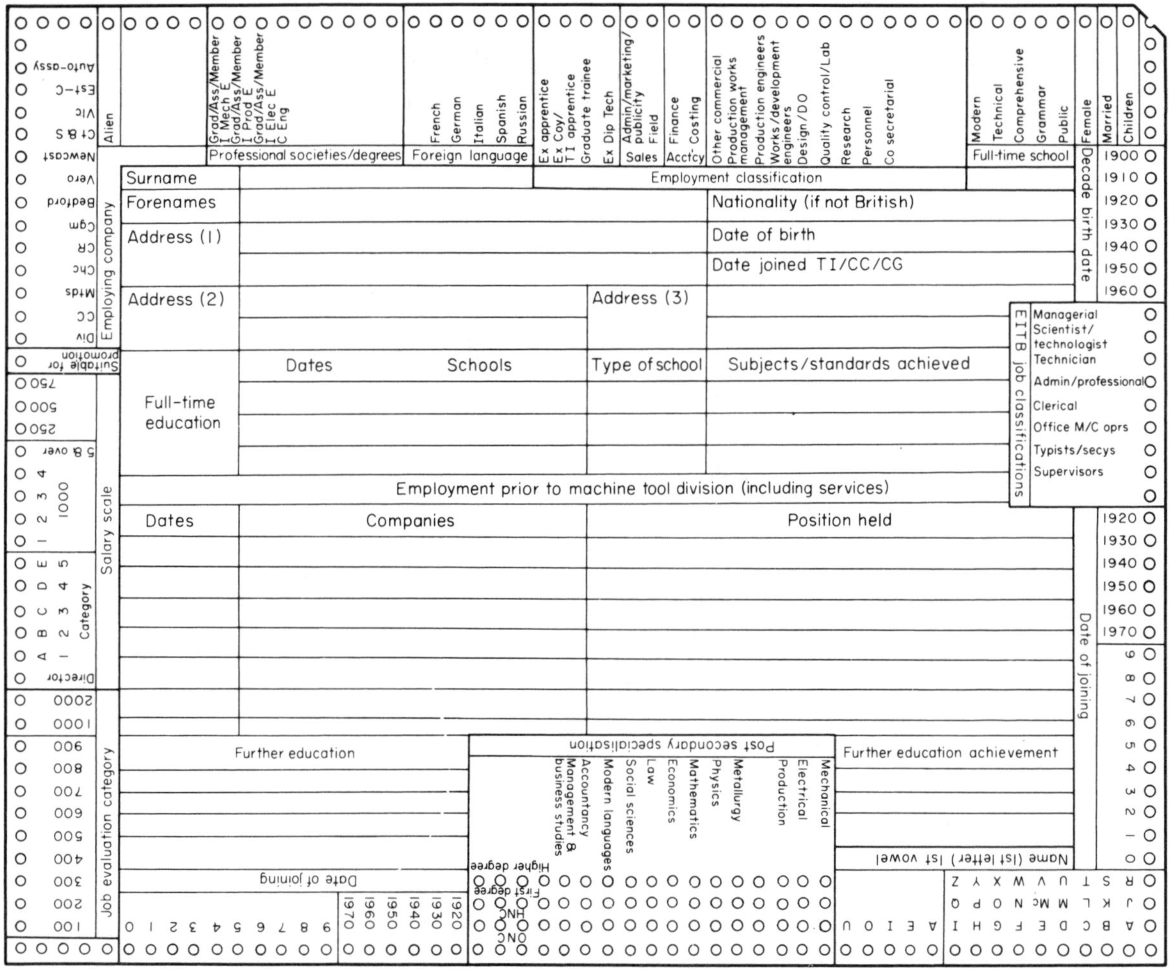

Figure 4:17 Notification of transfer or change

This is a four-copy set: one copy to the personnel department, one to the wages department, one to the timekeeper and one for filing (George Cohen 600 Group)

From _____

To (1) Wages Department

Employee's full name		Company	Depot

Item	Existing	Change to	Date	Remarks
Clock number				Not to be changed without reference to Wages Department
Department				
Occupation				
Rate of pay				If changed state reason
Other item				
Other item				

Signed _____ Foreman or Department Head   Date _____ Authorised _____ Works/Depot Manager

Figure 4:18   Staff transfer form
This type of form is used for departmental transfer (Greater London Council and
Inner London Education Authority)

CSF 150(W)

GREATER LONDON COUNCIL

INNER LONDON EDUCATION AUTHORITY

MEMORANDUM to

from   tel.   date
_____

STAFF TRANSFER

Mr/Mrs/Miss... Date of birth..

Private address...

.... Telephone..................................

has been transferred to your department from and including...
                                    _____

Grade.................................. Date attained.......................... Incremental date..

Weekly rate of pay... Income tax code...

Taxable pay to date... Tax paid to date.......................................

Wages paid up to.......................... If paid by computer, week number of transfer..

Superannuation number...................... Rate... Contracted out/Participating

Arrears outstanding...

NI classification.................................. NI contributions:— Council..

                                    Employee..

Previous year's gross income (if known)..

Graduated NI:— Contracted out/Participating   Rate..

Particulars of service (including details of previous public service):

Sick leave entitlement.. RDP: Yes/No

Particulars of sick leave during last 12 months:

Annual leave entitlement.............................. Rising to.................... Leave outstanding on transfer..

Further information (to include relevant details of special leave, discipline charges, extended sickness, special allowances, etc.)

Insurance card attached/to follow/with Treasurer   Personal file attached/to follow

P.45 attached/to follow/with Treasurer   ACR's attached/to follow

P 3450/cc 458

Figure 4:19   Personnel data amendment form (Twinlock Group)

Confidential   Please complete in block capitals. Delete sections not applicable

To Group Personnel Services   Please note the following
                                                amendment(s) and take the
                                                necessary action

		Clock number
Name	Mr Mrs Miss	
		Department/company
Job title		
		Cost centre

1   New employee (GPS use only)

Date of starting	Hours of work	Date of birth	Rate of pay	Per	Bonus/ merit	Per
				Year Week Hour		Year Week Hour
National Insurance card received and number					P45 received	

2   Transfer

Date of transfer	Department/cost centre		New job title	
	From	To		

Is there a change in pay and/or status?   Yes/No
If Yes complete section 3 below

3   Wage/ salary/ status/ change

Date effective	Present rate	New rate	Regrading	
			From	To

4   Termination

Date of leaving	Leaving code	Holiday days outstanding (staff only)	Would you re-employ?
			Yes/No

Authorisation

_____   _____
            Manager   Date
_____   _____
   Divisional Head (where applicable)   Group Personnel Services

Figure 4:20 Journal or day book

These standard sheets are of toughened paper to withstand regular use and are perforated to go into a ring binder. The serial number on the engagement register is continuous and thus indicates the number of movements over any period. Department numbers and employee personal numbers are allotted in the categories of men, full-time women, part-time women, and are used to show movements that have taken place either in a department or in a main category of employee

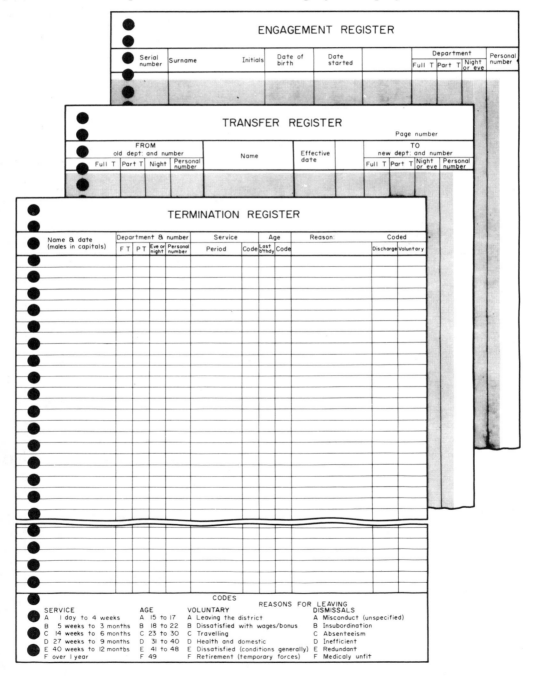

5

Health, Safety and Absenteeism

The Health and Safety at Work etc. Act 1974 brought considerable changes to the safety requirements within companies. Medical and accident records are required by law, but extensive arrangements for recording data beyond the demands of the law are well worth while provided constructive use is made of the data.

The requirement to consult with safety representatives has meant that safety procedures and records are essential. The Act seeks not only to simplify and strengthen the present legislation protecting people at work but also to protect members of the public who might be affected by the activities of the workforce. In order to identify potential hazards in all areas and thereby the need for new safety practices, many companies have introduced methods of recording and analysing information to cover their own special requirements. Particularly dangerous practices are often preceded by an 'authorisation to work' form where an employee is given the authority to commence work on a particular piece of equipment either *a*) because he has special skills or knowledge or *b*) because the equipment has been cleared for safe usage. Figure 5:1 shows such a form.

Medical Records

Most firms which have a full-time medical officer, a regular visiting doctor or a full-time nurse, keep individual employee medical records for all employees. In other firms, a record is raised only when an employee sees the medical officer for the first time. Figure 5:2 shows an example of a medical record.

How complete such records should be, must, of course, depend on the objectives of the medical department. It could simply be a place for first-aid treatment. If it is providing a comprehensive occupational health service, its efficiency will depend on an adequate medical history of each employee. Basic facts will be collected by the nurse at the first interview – possibly on the occasion of a medical examination –

before the employee starts work, and additional information of a medical diagnostic nature will be completed by the medical officer.

The medical history record should be designed so that additional information can be added from time to time. It is possible to have two parts: the confidential information completed by and available to the medical officer and nurse only, and routine information which can be completed by a clerk.

As the relationship between a doctor and a patient depends on mutual confidence, it is advisable to inform employees on engagement how medical reports are used and by whom they are seen. It may be assumed that where a doctor is employed it is to look after the interests and health of employees, and that any report which includes a statement of ailment will be submitted to the employer by the doctor without breaking the confidence between patient and doctor.

Medical history forms and medical examinations

A number of companies require that every prospective employee has a medical examination. In other firms it is only necessary for him to complete a brief form giving his medical history in order to determine whether or not a medical examination should be given. Figure 5:3 is an example of such a form. Some firms include the medical history form on their applications, particularly where health is an important factor in selection. (See Figure 2:8.)

In certain industries, employees must be examined before starting work and then periodically. If a physical examination is required before acceptance, this fact should be stated in the recruitment advertisements or at least on the application form.

By law, no person under the age of eighteen may be taken into employment in a factory for more than fourteen days without notice being given by the factory occupier to the local careers office of the Youth Employment Service. The careers office can consult the School Health Service records and can consult the employment medical adviser for the area who may veto a particular employment that is medically unsuitable.

Day book

Every visit to the first-aid or medical section should be recorded in a 'day book' which should contain the following details:

1   Date
2   Time
3   Name
4   Sex
5   Department and number
6   Reason for attendance
7   Details of treatment

The day book may be a bound register or a loose-leaf binder. It may have tear-off duplicate pages if a copy is needed for inspection by the medical officer or the personnel manager. Where it is agreed that the day book is available for information to the line or personnel manager, it will be for the staff of the medical department to decide which information is confidential and should be recorded separately.

As an alternative to the day book, a system of notes can be used. These are originated by the supervisor and taken by the employee to the nurse who keeps the main portion in which she records the usual day-book details. The torn-off section may be returned to the supervisor for his information or given to the employee to remind him of his next appointment.

In smaller firms, or in those where treatment is usually given by first-aiders at the place of work, duplicate tear-off sheets are probably the most satisfactory type of day book as the duplicates can be dispatched daily to the personnel department, or in the case of accidents, to the safety officer. If perforated slips are not used, the personnel manager or the safety officer may receive information only sporadically – for example, when a page is completed. On the other hand, it is possible for the tear-off sheets to be mislaid.

Accident Records and Reports

It is essential that details of accidents are reported to the personnel department and that reports are kept for insurance purposes to meet claims under common law liability as well as to meet statutory obligations.

Comprehensive records of accidents, based on accurate observation, are also essential to any programme designed to reduce accidents. It is important that accident records are kept for each individual to identify those who are accident prone, the psychological and mental stresses of particular jobs and to indicate training needs.

Figure 5:4 shows the accident record card recommended by the Royal Society for the Prevention of Accidents (RoSPA) from whom copies are available at a minimal cost. On the reverse side of the record card is a standard classification of accidents. An edge-punched card is used so that statistical analyses can be carried out.

Requirements of the report

An accident report should be completed for every accident as soon as possible after it happens, before memory fades. Normally, the immediate line supervisor, but sometimes the safety officer, will originate the report, though some of the personal details may have to be completed by the personnel department. It is normal practice in most firms for the works manager, the personnel officer and the safety representative to be informed immediately by telephone of any serious accident. In some firms duplicate copies are raised to speed the process.

Reports of accidents will be needed by a number of people:

The safety officer, or whoever is responsible for safety, will need the information as the basis of his investigations and for his statistical return or analyses.

Management need the information in order to take steps to avoid similar accidents.

The insurance company with which the firm insures against common law liability may have to be informed.

HM inspector of health and safety at work may require notification on statutory form 43.

The Department of Health and Social Security form relating to industrial injuries will need to be completed if the employee claims that the accident happened at work.

Safety committee of the firm will expect details.

The details required by these different bodies will vary. It is therefore advisable to have an accident report form which is comprehensive. The items of information most frequently asked for on accident forms are:

1   Name, clock number, sex, age, occupation
2   Address, married or single, children under sixteen, weekly earnings (completed by personnel officer if employee loses time)
3   Date and time of accident
4   Date and time accident reported
5   Date and time injured employee stopped work as a result of the accident
6   Time he started work on day or night of accident
7   Number of hours of continuous employment before accident
8   Cause of accident
9   What exactly was employee doing at the time (in detail)
10 Was he authorised or permitted to do what he was doing?
11 If the accident was due to machinery state:
    (*a*) Name of machine and part causing accident
    (*b*) Whether in motion by mechanical power at the time of the accident
12 Nature and extent of injury, stating exact part of body affected
13 State whether employee received treatment at:
    (*a*) First-aid box (state which)
    (*b*) Ambulance room
    (*c*) Hospital (state which)
    (*d*) Own doctor (state name)
14 Name and clock number(s) of any person(s) who witnessed the accident

15 Was personal protective clothing or equipment necessary for the work being done at the time of the accident. If so:
   (*a*) Was it provided?
   (*b*) Was it being used?
16 Written statements from witnesses are often requested on the accident form and space is allowed for observations and other relevant information
17 An office section checklist is sometimes included covering:
   (*a*) Form F43 sent to factory inspector
   (*b*) Entry in accident book checked
18 Entry in general register (form 31A) recorded
19 Department of Health and Social Security claim form received
20 Employer's liability insurance form sent
21 Reported to accident prevention committee
22 Date employee returned to work
23 Number of days lost
24 Any disablement on return

Some firms have a section for recommendations on action to be taken to avoid similar accidents. It is advantageous to consult workers and ask their advice about any proposed changes.

Figures 5:5 and 5:6 show examples of accident report forms. Some time after an accident or illness it may be necessary to consider the redeployment of the employee involved, whether it be permanent or temporary redeployment, and in these circumstances certain background information will be required. Figure 5:7 shows a checklist of relevant information.

Medical and Accident Statistics

Medical and accident records form the basis for a variety of statistics of interest to employers, and may help to determine certain positive correlations between working conditions and health. Again, the analysis to be carried out will be determined by the size of the unit and the industry.

Medical returns

Some firms analyse sickness absence by cause. There are several difficulties. For example, a doctor is not bound to state on a medical certificate to his patient's employer the exact nature of an illness; moreover, it is possible for an employee to be suffering from more than one complaint, only one of which may be mentioned. Also, an illness may start as one complaint but develop into another. The National Insurance certificate may give more information and in many cases the employee sends his certificate to his employer who forwards it to the appropriate DHSS office, having noted the diagnosis.

Medical statistics

A large firm will have sufficient numbers of sickness absences every year to derive a useful general picture of the most common illnesses within the firm and of year-to-year trends. A reason can be sought if these vary from such few national figures for comparable groups of people as are available – the Department of Health and Social Security's *Digest of Statistics Analysing Certificates of Incapacity*, for example.

Few statistics are more open to misinterpretation than medical ones. Many independent variables must be considered. The most important are the age and sex structure of the employee population and their marital status. The hours of work, shift system, sick-pay scheme, geographical location of the firm, length of weekend, and many other factors will each have some influence. Clearly, this is a specialist field in which the layman must tread warily. But this does not absolve management from all interest in this important matter.

The experience of large companies with full-scale medical centres, or of small companies with access to group centres, indicates that getting immediate treatment at work reduces absence from work because of time spent attending a doctor or hospital for treatment. Medical supervision of workers who have been absent, as well as the long-term benefits of better health and morale, more than cover the annual recurring costs of the centres. Increasing emphasis in industrial medicine is now being placed on preventive measures; for example, occupational hygiene, the investigation of potentially hazardous working conditions, and ergonomics – the study of man at work with the aim of ensuring that the task required of any operator is within his capacity and makes the best use of his abilities.

Accident statistics

Comparison of the current accident return with earlier returns will help to discover trends, and may pinpoint particular types of injury which are on the increase.

Comparisons of one firm's progress with another demand some common yardstick. The two which are generally recognised are the 'frequency rate' and the 'mean duration' rate.

The frequency rate is the rate at which accidents occur. It is expressed as the number of lost-time accidents per 100 000 man-hours worked:

$$\frac{\text{number of lost-time accidents} \times 100\ 000}{\text{man-hours worked}}$$

A 'lost-time accident' is defined as one which prevents an employee continuing his normal duties beyond the end of the day or shift in which the accident occurs. An accident which causes an employee to be transferred to a light job, because of an injury, should therefore be included.

Sometimes an accident does not result in lost time immediately, but causes the employee to lose time later. It should be included in the frequency rate for the period when it causes loss of time. If an accident causes intermittent absence – a day off a week for treatment, for example – it should be included in the frequency rate only when the first loss of time occurs.

In an industry with few hazards the accident frequency rate should be less than one and should be below two or three in even the most hazardous industries. These figures normally relate to manual workers only as the proportion of office workers varies radically from firm to firm. The industrial safety division of RoSPA publishes a survey annually showing both the frequency rate and the mean duration rate of a large number of firms scheduled according to industry.

In firms with less than 1000 employees the figure yielded by the accident frequency formula on a monthly basis may fluctuate violently and only annual results will be significant. A moving average covering five or six months will show the degree of progress.

Mean duration rate is the arithmetical mean of the time lost due to accidents and is expressed as follows:

$$\frac{\text{number of man-hours lost}}{\text{number of lost-time accidents}}$$

A 'lost-time accident' is defined in the same way as under the frequency rate, but fatalities are excluded.

Nature of injury

A regular analysis of injuries will help to show any sudden increase which calls for action. The recommended breakdown is as follows:

1   Open wounds and lacerations
2   Bruising with intact skin and concussion
3   Foreign bodies in various sites
4   Crushing injuries
5   Sprains and strains
6   Fractures and dislocations
7   Internal injuries
8   Burns
9   Nerve injuries
10 Traumatic amputations
11 Concussion
12 Asphyxiation or poisoning by gas or fume
13 Asphyxiation other than by gas or fume
14 Poisoning other than by gas or fume
15 Electric shock

Accident returns

The accident return form will assist management in their investigation of each particular accident, but something more general is needed to assist further in the reduction of accidents.

Periodic returns, monthly, quarterly or annually, giving the total number of accidents in the factory are normal and they are usually analysed according to the department, the type of accident and the part of the body injured.

Some overlapping with the accident returns of the safety officer may be inevitable, and there will be some duplication with the general register and accident register, but a great deal of valuable information can be collected from the medical department day book. The main figures indicate what proportion of the total visits to the surgery are because of accidents compared with illness.

The 'type of accident' analysis usually follows the schedule below which is taken from a report by HM Chief Inspector of Factories:

Primary cause of accident (factories only)
1 Power-driven machinery
2 Non-power machinery
3 Transport
4 Fires and explosions of combustible material
5 Explosions of pressure vessels
6 Falls of persons
7 Due to electricity
8 Poisoning and gassing
9 Stepping on or striking against objects
10 Struck by falling objects
11 Handling goods
12 Use of hand tools
13 Miscellaneous

Accident figures can also be divided into those which happened at work and those which happened at home, and into first attendances and re-dressings. The number of employees examined by the medical officer, referred to hospital, or sent home, may be of interest. An analysis of the nature of the injury may also be included.

Part of body affected. An analysis of which parts of the body have been injured may also be included. This will help to focus attention on the need for stricter supervision of the wearing of protective clothing, such as goggles, spats, helmets or boots, or on the need for instruction in correct methods of manual lifting and handling.

The schedule included in the standard form produced by the industrial division of the Royal Society for the Prevention of Accidents is as follows:

1	Head and neck	12	Toes
2	Eyes	13	Shoulder
3	Back and spinal column	14	Arm
4	Chest	15	Elbow
5	Abdomen	16	Forearm
6	Buttock and pelvis	17	Wrist
7	Thigh	18	Hand
8	Knee	19	Fingers
9	Leg	20	Thumb
10	Ankle	21	Non-localised internal
11	Foot		

Obligatory Reports

Under the Factories Act 1961 a record of any accident that prevents an employee from earning full wages at his normal job for more than three days, any 'industrial disease' (defined in regulations) or 'dangerous occurrence' (defined in regulations) is required to be entered into the general register.

Accidents causing loss of life or disabling a worker for more than three days must also be reported immediately to the district inspector of factories. Figure 5:8 shows form F43 which must be used in all cases except where the accident or dangerous occurrence happens in the course of building operations or works of engineering construction. If the accident is fatal, HM factory inspector must be informed immediately in writing.

In premises covered by the Offices, Shops and Railway Premises Act, a different form, shown in Figure 5:9 should be used.

In addition, the Department of Health and Social Security form relating to industrial injuries must be completed if the employee claims that the accident happened at work.

Industrial diseases must also be entered in the general register and reported immediately to the District Inspector of Factories and to the employment medical adviser for the area. The official form for reporting these, as prescribed by The Notice of Industrial Diseases Order 1973, is shown in Figure 5:10.

Accident book

Every employer who normally employs ten or more people is obliged to keep an accident book in every factory, mine or quarry. It must be readily accessible at all reasonable times to any injured employee to enter particulars of any accident which has happened to him at work. These entries should be made in ink.

This book is intended to assist an injured person to give notice of his accident to his employer as required by the National Insurance (Industrial Injuries) Acts. An entry in this book, if made as soon as practicable after the accident occurred, is sufficient notice of the accident for the purpose of these Acts.

In offices and other premises not covered by the Factories Act 1961 it is advisable for the employer to maintain a copy of form OSR2 so that a record of reportable accidents is maintained by the firm. Accident books should be retained permanently.

Insurance Claims

The National Insurance (Industrial Injuries) Acts regulate a scheme of insurance that provides compensation for physical or mental personal injuries arising 'out of or in the course of ' employment.

Besides giving notice of the accident the worker must also make a claim to his employer for compensation within six months. Claims in respect of death must be made within six months from the date of death. If the claim is not made within this period, proceedings for the recovery of compensation will be barred unless it is found that the failure to make the claim within the prescribed time was because of a mistake, absence from the UK or other reasonable cause.

After the notice of an accident has been given and the claim for compensation made, the workman must, if so required by the employer, submit himself for examination by a doctor provided and paid by the employer.

All claims for compensation may be settled by agreement between employer and workman, and the compensation may be paid by the employer direct to the workman.

If the claim is settled by agreement, a memorandum of the terms of the agreement must be sent to the registrar of the county court (in Scotland, the sheriff clerk) for registration. When registered, the agreement becomes enforceable as a county court judgement. In cases where an agreement is made, either in the first instance or subsequently, for payment of a lump sum instead of weekly payments, the agreement will not relieve the employer of his liability to make weekly payments unless the agreement has been registered.

Absenteeism

In many companies, a list of those who were late or absent is provided to a central office, usually Personnel, by each departmental supervisor or a designated clerk in each department. It may be preferable to make a list of absentees not on a daily basis, but weekly. The departmental head can then carry forward, from week to week, a running total of days lost by each absentee, so that either he or Personnel can take appropriate action after absence of a certain length. The reason for absence can be inserted by the supervisor when the employee returns to work. Figure 5:11 shows an example of a weekly report of absences.

In factories, a list of absentees and latecomers can be obtained from the current clock cards. Where separate 'in' and 'out' clock racks are maintained, this can be done quickly. In order to make sure that the employee reports to his supervisor on returning, the absentee's clock card is sometimes replaced by one of a different colour which he uses to clock in and then hands to his supervisor in return for his normal clock card. The supervisor then records the reason for the absence on the special card, which is then replaced in the clock card until collected by the person responsible for absence recording.

Alternatively, the clock cards can be obtained from the wages department when it has finished with them. The virtue of this arrangement is that the departmental supervisor will usually have checked the clock cards before the timekeeper received them and will have had an opportunity to discover the reason for the absence or lateness and to mark it on the card. The weakness of this system is that it fails to give a day-to-day figure, and fails to give a broad picture of absences or time lost throughout each department.

Many companies have made a works rule that all employees arriving late without previous written permission have to fill in and sign a 'reason for lateness' form. While such forms are not particularly effective, employees can be required under employment contract to sign these and can be suspended for breach of discipline if they fail to do so.

Absence records

It is usually advisable to record absences for each individual. This provides a complete record of the employee's absences and shows any regular pattern such as Monday absences, for example. It may be advantageous to link the recording of absences with the records used in the wages department to ensure accuracy.

Ideally, absence records should contain both absences and time lost, either because of lateness or leaving early, and the reasons. Figures 5:12 and 5:13 show two examples of such records. The form illustrated in Figure 5:14 includes a monthly summary on the reverse side.

Attendance records can be combined with the personal history records. Figure 5:15 shows a personal record with an overriding sheet which contains absences because of illness, as well as holidays and special leave. The combined personal data and attendance record shown in Figure 5:16 is notable for its simplicity and conciseness. The absenteeism record is on a split insert card which is printed on both sides alike and would, therefore, last a considerable time. Absenteeism is coded and each employee has a signal over one of the spaces *A*, *B* or *C* on the visible edge to indicate how prone he is to lateness.

Absence reports

A distinction normally has to be made between information necessary to record the trend of sickness absence over a period in one large department and information required to make comparisons between one working group and another.

Analyses of absenteeism and timekeeping records are useful for obtaining accurate information on the extent of this problem in one particular department or organisation. If sufficient information is provided they enable comparisons to be made between one group and another.

The simple recording of percentages of working time lost will indicate the trend of sickness absence over a period in a large department which has a fairly stable population. The gross absence rate for the firm is expressed as a percentage of planned production time, according to one of the following formulas:

$$\frac{\text{number of man-hours lost} \times 100}{\text{total number of possible hours}}$$

$$\frac{\text{number of half-days lost} \times 100}{\text{total number of possible half-days}}$$

Very little difference will result from these two methods. Overtime can cause tedious calculations in the case of the first formula; it would seem simplest to omit it altogether. Overtime is, however, a definite cause of absence, so some indication of the amount of overtime worked should be included on the individual record card and checked against the absence rate whenever it is worked out. Whenever short-time is worked it should be noted in the same way, as it will tend to reduce absence.

Considerable distortion of results can be caused by long-term absence. Such absence should be omitted after a certain time – usually thirteen weeks. Some firms omit it after four weeks but no interfirm comparison is of any value unless this period is the same and thirteen weeks is the recommended period.

The recording of percentages of working-time lost is useful, but more information can be obtained if the data are plotted on a graph so as to reveal long-term trends which might otherwise be imperceptible.

Changes in the total absence rate can be accounted for by some well-known factors. If these are not applicable, and the sickness-absence rate continues to rise, it may be necessary to use more detailed analyses to establish that there is a time increase in sickness absence caused, perhaps, by lowered morale, a change in environment or a change in work methods. Precautions must be taken in dealing with small numbers of employees since random fluctuations may occur because of the numerical size of the group. It may be necessary to collect the information for several years before a stable figure is reached which can be used.

In many companies, employees with a reasonable length of service who then have a protracted illness are transferred to a suspense register. This is kept by the personnel department and the employee is removed from the budget charge of his own department though still considered as a company employee. Pension contributions cease but the pension entitlement is not lost; the employee may be expected to make up the arrears of pension on return. Once on the suspense register a person does not figure on the absence returns.

The following factors should be taken into consideration in compiling absenteeism records:

1 If the composition of the working group is not stable, changes in the absence rate may be explained by a correlation *with age*. If older men replace younger ones there may be an increase in the rate. Men aged sixty to sixty-five may have twice the average number of spells of absence a year as men aged twenty-five to thirty. Older men may have four times the average number of days of absence in a year as younger men.

If the converse is happening there will be a higher incidence of short uncertified spells. It is common for firms not to require a medical certificate for the first three days of absence. As the casual absentee may cause most disruption to an organisation, it is necessary to record and analyse short uncertified absences separately from the long.

2 Another factor is the incidence of *epidemics* which may cause the figures for one year to be misleading.

3 The effects of the introduction of *sick-pay schemes* vary considerably. It is not necessarily true that people getting sick pay have a higher rate of absence. This depends very much upon the type of occupation and the traditions of the group as well as how suddenly the scheme is introduced.

Records necessary for comparative studies

If records are to be kept so that comparisons may be made between factories in differing localities or between different working groups, there are additional factors that vary widely and have to be taken into account.

Occupation. This has different effects on absence rates; a disease which may prevent a person in one type of job from going to work may not seriously incapacitate someone in another.

Where people live and work. The significance of this is great. Those who live and work in industrial areas have a higher sickness absence rate than those who work in rural areas. It is possible to show, too, that certain metropolitan districts show a greater incidence of respiratory diseases which is then reflected in absence records.

Type of illness. A difference in the type of illness affecting two groups must be allowed for, as some illnesses naturally produce shorter lengths of absence than others. It is necessary to use both the indexes of frequency and duration to make the difference apparent.

Causes of absence. It is seldom worth while or even possible when preparing a company-wide analysis to give the cause of absence in greater detail than the following:

1 Sickness (including external accidents)
2 Accidents at work
3 Other absence with permission
4 Other absence without permission

Some firms also record holidays on individual absence records, usually when holidays are staggered. The type of illness is sometimes recorded and this, with the problems involved, are discussed a bit further. Large firms can derive much useful information from an analysis of absence according to type of illness; even small firms may find an indication that working conditions in some departments are inadequate.

Probably the most useful source of information is the day book. Much can be learned from a well-kept day book, both about hazards in the different departments of the factory and about employees. The pattern of pressure on the department will become clear, indicating the most convenient times for appointments to be made for such things as re-dressings.

Some firms like to analyse statistically all visits to the first-aid or medical section as it is felt, for instance, that this will give a more comprehensive picture of the extent of minor injuries. The weakness here is that attendance may reflect merely the amount of encouragement or discouragement given by the supervisor to employees who wish to attend the medical department.

Accidents may be separated from medical treatments and re-dressings in the day book by using either separate columns, different coloured inks, or by splitting them between the top and bottom halves of the page. This facilitates statistical work which can be further eased by the daily totalling and recording of attendances at the bottom of each page.

N.B. The Health and Safety Commission is proposing regulations at the present time which it is hoped will come into operation on 1 January 1980. These regulations will change both the system of notifying accidents and dangerous occurrences and the forms which will be used for that purpose.

Figure 5:1 Permit to work form

For use on electrical equipment with three copies, colour coded for circulation to the relevant departments (Greater London Council)

GREATER LONDON COUNCIL

PERMIT-TO-WORK ON ELECTRICAL APPARATUS

Nº 19005

OTHER RELEVANT PERMIT

Nos.

KEY SAFE No.

1. ISSUE

To

In the employ of

For the following work to be carried out:

I hereby declare that it is safe to work on the following apparatus which is switched out, isolated from all live conductors and is connected to earth.

ALL OTHER PARTS ARE DANGEROUS

Circuit mains earths have been connected at the following points.

Danger or Caution notices have been posted at

Special Precautions taken

Signed

being an Authorised Person possessing Authority to issue a Permit-to-Work in accordance with the Electrical Safety Rules.

Time Date

2. RECEIPT

Note: After Part 1 has been signed this receipt must be signed by and the Permit retained by the Person in charge of the work until the work is suspended or completed.

I hereby declare that I accept responsibility for carrying out work on the apparatus detailed on this Permit, and that no attempt will be made by me or by any man under my control to carry out work on any other apparatus.

Signed , being the person in charge of the work.

Time Date

3. CLEARANCE

Note: The apparatus mentioned hereon must not be recommissioned until this clearance has been signed and the Permit returned by the person in charge of the work and Part 4 completed.

I hereby declare that the work for which this permit was issued is now completed*/suspended* and that all men under my charge have been withdrawn and warned that it is no longer safe to work on the apparatus specified in this Permit, and that all gear, tools and temporary earth connections are clear.

Signed , being the person in charge of the work.

Time Date

4. CANCELLATION

Note: This portion must not be completed before Part 3 has been completed. I hereby declare this Permit-to-Work cancelled and the earth connections specified in Part 1 have been removed.

Signed being an Authorised Person.

Time Date

* Delete the word that does not apply.

300×50×3 (S×P13161·P471931 9/72

Figure 5:2   Employee medical history card
The reverse side has space for notes on attendance at the works surgery

CONFIDENTIAL **EMPLOYEE MEDICAL HISTORY** (NOT TO BE TAKEN FROM WORKS HOSPITAL)	DATE OF BIRTH	CHRISTIAN NAMES		SURNAME
ADDRESS	CHANGE OF ADDRESS (DELETE OLD)		IF MEMBER OF: FIRE BRIGADE FIRST AID	DATE SERVICE COUNTS FROM
PREVIOUS HEALTH RECORD			IF DISABLED, REGISTRATION No	DATE SERVICE TERMINATES

MEDICAL EXAMINATIONS

DATE	CLOCK NUMBER	JOB	EXAMINATION				WORKS DOCTOR'S REMARKS
			STAT OR C P	HEIGHT	WEIGHT	VISION	

Figure 5:3 Medical history form (Marconi Company Limited)

| Name _____ Date of birth _____ |
| Department _____ |
| Occupation _____ |

Please answer yes or no to all the following questions		For surgery use only. Remarks
Do you suffer from, or have you ever had : –		
Heart trouble of any kind		
Lung trouble (including tuberculosis)		
Nervous trouble (including fainting attacks, fits or nervous breakdown)		
Abdominal trouble		
Skin disease		
Eye trouble		
Ear trouble		
Rupture or varicose veins		
An accident with after effects		
Any other disease, disability or operation		
Has your chest been X–rayed, if so, when and with what result		
Have you lived abroad, if so, where and when		
Are you a registered disabled person		
If so, please state (*a*) Registration card number		
(*b*) Date of expiry		

To the best of my knowledge and belief, the information I have given above is correct

Signature _____ Date _____

The information asked for is required in the interests of the employee or prospective employee

On request, an interview with the medical officer will be arranged as an alternative to completing the form or to supplement the information given

Figure 5:4   Accident record card

This form is available from the Royal Society for the Prevention of Accidents. It was designed to facilitate statistical analyses

---

THE ROYAL SOCIETY FOR THE PREVENTION OF ACCIDENTS

(INDUSTRIAL SAFETY DIVISION)

RoSPA

ACCIDENT RECORD CARD

NAME _____ CLOCK No. _____

WORKS _____

BRANCH/DEPT. _____ (No. _____) TRADE _____ (No. _____)

DATE ___ / ___ / 19 _____ TIME _____

ACCIDENT LOCATION _____

BRIEF REPORT _____

SEX — MALE / FEMALE

AGE (YEARS):
16 – 17
17 – 18
18 – 21
22 – 25
26 – 30
31 – 35
36 – 40
41 – 45
46 – 50
51 – 55
56 – 60
61 – 65
65+

MONTHS OF SERVICE:
– 1
1 – 3
3 – 6
6 – 12

YEARS LENGTH OF SERVICE:
1 – 5
6 – 10
10+

METHOD OF PAYMENT:
TIME
PIECE
BONUS

TRADE — HUNDS. / TENS / UNITS

DEPARTMENT — TENS / UNITS

JOB EXPER. — UNDER / OVER

P.T.O.

CODES

MONTH	INJURY CAUSE	INJURY LOCATION	INJURY NATURE	INDUSTRIAL DISEASES

DAY WORK — 1ST. / 2ND. / 3RD. — OVERTIME

DAY/SHIFT OVERTIME

NATURE:
1. OPEN WOUNDS & LACERATIONS
2. BRUISING WITH INTACT SKIN
3. FOREIGN BODIES IN VARIOUS SITES
4. CRUSHING INJURIES
5. SPRAINS & STRAINS
6. FRACTURES & DISLOCATIONS
7. BURNS
8. NERVE INJURIES
9. TRAUMATIC AMPUTATIONS
10. CONCUSSION
11. ASPHYXIATION/POISONING BY GAS OR FUME
12. ASPHYXIATION OTHER THAN BY GAS OR FUME
13. POISONING OTHER THAN BY GAS OR FUME
14. ELECTRIC SHOCK

INJURY CAUSE:
21. NON-LOCALISED/INTERNAL
20. THUMB
19. FINGERS
18. HAND
17. WRIST
16. FOREARM
15. ELBOW
14. ARM
13. SHOULDER
12. FOOT
11. TOES
10. ANKLE
9. LEG
8. KNEE
7. THIGH
6. BUTTOCK & PELVIS
5. ABDOMEN
4. CHEST
3. BACK & SPINAL COLUMN
2. EYES
1. HEAD & NECK

INJURY NATURE / LOCATION:
12. MISCELLANEOUS
11. ANIMALS
10. HAND TOOLS
9. HANDLING OBJECTS
8. OBJECTS FALLING
7. STEPPING ON OR AGAINST STRIKING OBJECTS
6. FALLS OF PERSONS
5. ACCIDENTAL OCCUP...
4. POISONOUS & CORROSIVE SUBS.
3. HOT SUBSTANCES, FIRES
2. EXPLOSIVES, ELECTRICITY
1. MACHINERY
... VEHICLES

INJURY CAUSES

ACCIDENT CAUSES — DESIGN / SUPERVISION / PERSONAL

ACCIDENT CAUSE: SEPSIS — BEFORE / AFTER

	ACCIDENT LOCATION		
PERSONAL	SUPERVISION	DESIGN	
UNITS	UNITS	UNITS	TENS

15 14 13 12 11 10 9 8 7 6 5 4 3 2 1

Figure 5:5 Accident report form

This is the front page of the form. The other three pages are for reports of dangerous occurrences, poisoning or disease.

REPORT OF ACCIDENT CAUSING ABSENCE FROM WORK (to the Personnel Manager)

P T O for report of dangerous occurrences, poisoning, or disease

1   Address of factory _____ _____

2   Injured person's surname _____ Forenames _____

         Address _____

         Age _____ Occupation _____

3   Date and hour of accident _____

4   What time did the injured person cease work ? _____

5   How did the accident happen ? _____

6   If accident is due to lifting by hand state *(a)* Total weight of load lifted _____

                                  (b) How many others assisted with the lifting _____

7   If caused by machinery :

      (a) Give name of machine and part causing accident _____

      (b) State whether it was moved by mechanical power at the time _____

      (c) State exacty what the injured person was doing at the time _____

8   Nature and extent of the injuries _____

9   Has the accident been entered in the Departmental Accident Book ? _____ Signed ? _____

10   Has the employee notified the Department of Health and Social Security _____

11   *(a)* Was the injured person at his or her usual or proper place of work when the accident

          happened ? _____

      (b) If not, was the injured person doing something that he/she was authorised or permitted to do for

          the purposes of his/her work ? _____

12   Names of any persons who actually witnessed the accident _____

13   Name of Medical Attendant _____

14   If taken to hospital or home address _____

         Signed _____ Departmental Manager

         Department _____ Date _____

PERSONNEL RECORDS (giving dates of entries etc)

1 Entered in The General Register for Factories _____

2 H M District Inspector of Factories advised _____

3 Confirmed with the Department of Health and Social Security _____

4 Insurance Co advised _____

5 Entered in Personnel Accident Record Book _____

6 Reported to the Joint Industrial Council _____

Figure 5:6 Accident Report Form

This form has four sections, colour coded for circulation to different departments. Part A shows full details of the incident itself and Part B the casualty information (Greater London Council)

Figure 5:7   Redeployment of Unfit Staff – Checklist
This form is completed for inter-departmental use (Greater London Council)

GREATER LONDON COUNCIL   Ref: HE/AE
Department of Public Health Engineering   Ext: 4252
INTER DEPARTMENTAL TRANSFER UNIT
INFORMATION REQUIRED FOR CONSIDERING THE REDEPLOYMENT OF UNFIT
STAFF
 1 NAME
 2 DEPARTMENT
 3 GRADE
    DUTIES
 4 OFFICIAL ADDRESS
 5 HOME ADDRESS
 6 AGE
 7 PERMANENT/TEMPORARY
 8 REGISTERED DISABLED PERSON
 9 DATE OF ENTRY   PREVIOUS SERVICE
10 QUALIFICATIONS, PREVIOUS JOBS,
    PERSONAL CIRCUMSTANCES ETC.

11 CALIBRE OF SERVICE
12 DETAILS OF ILLNESS OR ACCIDENT

13 RESTRICTIONS ON ABILITIES AND
    PROSPECTS FOR CONTINUED EMPLOYMENT

14 DETAILS OF PRESENT PAY
15 DETAILS OF SICK PAY ENTITLEMENT
16 ENTITLED TO GRATUITY/PENSION
17 SPECIAL APTITUDES: SUGGESTIONS
    FOR FUTURE WORK

18 RESULT OF M.A.'s EXAMINATION
19 VACANCIES TRIED

Figure 5:8   Notice of accident or dangerous occurrence (F43)
Page 1 of the form that should be sent to HM Inspector of Factories immediately the accident or dangerous occurrence becomes reportable under the Factories Act. Copies of the form may be bought from Her Majesty's Stationery Office

---

HEALTH AND SAFETY EXECUTIVE   F 43
HM FACTORY INSPECTORATE   Reprinted November 1977

A notice in this form should be sent to HM Inspector of Factories immediately the accident or dangerous occurrence becomes reportable. (See instruction overleaf.) If the accident is fatal, HM Inspector should be informed immediately in writing.

FACTORIES ACT 1961, sections 80 and 81 and the
Dangerous Occurrences (Notification) Regulations 1947
Prescribed form of written notice of
ACCIDENT OR DANGEROUS OCCURRENCE

NOTE: For accidents occurring:
(a) on building operations or works of engineering construction, use form F43B.
(b) in offices or shops; use form OSR2.

FOR OFFICIAL USE
District and date of receipt

No. of copies required

1 (a) OCCUPIER of factory (or person carrying on processes at Docks, and certain other places).	MR Group
Name	Ref to
Address	M of T, etc
Industry	1 Serial No.
(b) Actual employer of injured person if other than above	2 M W B G
Name	3
Address	4 F, NF, DO
2 PLACE where accident or dangerous occurrence happened:	4(a)
(a) Address (if different from 1(a) above)	4(b)
(b) Exact location	5 Process
(c) Nature of work carried on there	6 SIC
3 INJURED PERSON	7(a) Causation
(a) Full name (surname first)	7(b)
(b) Sex.............. Age..............	7(c)
(c) Address	7(d)
(d) Occupation	7(e)
4 ACCIDENT or DANGEROUS OCCURRENCE	7(f)
(a) Date.................... Time....................	7(g)
(b) Full details of how the accident or dangerous occurrence happened and what injured person was doing. If a fall of a person or materials, plant, etc state height of fall (if necessary continue on separate sheet).	7(h)
	7(j)
	7(k)
(c) If due to machinery, state:	7(l)
(i) Name and type of machine	8 Occupation
(ii) Part causing injury................	9 Injury Nature Site
(iii) Whether in motion by mechanical power at the time................	10
(iv) If caused by crane or other lifting machine, specify type................	11
5 INJURIES AND DISABLEMENT	12
(a) Nature and extent of injury (eg fracture of leg, laceration of arm, scalded foot, scratch on hand followed by sepsis)................	13

    (b) Whether fatal or non-fatal................

    (c) Was injured person disabled for more than three days from earning full wages at the work at which he was employed?................

6 Has accident (or dangerous occurrence) been entered in the General Register?................

    Signature of Occupier, Employer, or Agent................   Date................

(Please see overleaf)

Figure 5:9 Notice of accident (OSR2)

Page 1 of the form prescribed by the Department of Employment for accidents in premises covered by the Offices, Shops and Railway Premises Act. Copies of the form may be bought from Her Majesty's Stationery Office

---

HEALTH AND SAFETY EXECUTIVE

OSR 2

OFFICES, SHOPS AND RAILWAY PREMISES ACT 1963

Notice of Accident

Form prescribed by the Secretary of State for Employment
for the purpose of section 48 of the
Offices, Shops and Railway Premises Act 1963

FOR OFFICIAL USE
Enforcing Authority and Date of Receipt

	1 Serial No.
1 OCCUPIER OF PREMISES	
(a) Name	2 MWBG
Address	
Nature of business	3 Workplace
(b) Actual employer of injured person if other than above	
Name	4(a) Causation
Address	
2 INJURED PERSON	4(b)
(a) Full Name *(Surname first)* Mr./Mrs./Miss	
(b) Age Occupation	4(c)
(c) Address	
3 PLACE WHERE ACCIDENT HAPPENED	4(d)
(a) Address *(if different from 1 (a) above)*	
(b) Exact location *(e.g. staircase to office; canteen storeroom; shop counter)*	
4 ACCIDENT	5(a) Injury
(a) Date Time	F N/F
(b) Full details of how the accident happened and what injured person was doing. If a fall of person or materials, plant, etc. state height of fall *(if necessary continue overleaf)*.	5(b) Nature of Injury
	5(c) Site of Injury
	6
	7
(c) If due to machinery, state:	
(i) Name and type of machine	8
(ii) What part of the machine caused the accident?	
(iii) Was the machine in motion by mechanical power at the time?	9
5 INJURIES AND DISABLEMENT	
(a) Whether fatal or non-fatal	10
(b) Nature and extent of injury *(e.g. fracture of leg, laceration of arm, scalded foot, scratch on hand followed by sepsis)*	
	11
Signature of Occupier or Agent Date	

NOTES: 1 A notice in this form should be sent to the appropriate authority as soon as the accident becomes reportable, i.e. when the injured person has been disabled FOR MORE THAN THREE DAYS FROM DOING HIS USUAL WORK; if the accident is fatal the appropriate authority should be informed immediately in writing. (See more detailed notes overleaf).

2 Accidents occurring in places subject to the Factories Act should be reported on form F43 to HM Factory Inspectorate.

Figure 5:10   Notice of case of poisoning or disease (F41)
This form must be completed and sent to The District Inspector of Factories and the Employment Medical Adviser for the area. Copies of the form may be bought from Her Majesty's Stationery Office

Health & Safety Executive

HM Factory Inspectorate

Form prescribed by the Secretary of State   F 41

Notice of case of poisoning or disease

occurring in a factory or in other premises or places to which the provisions of section 82(3) and (4) of the Factories Act 1961 apply

This box to be filled in by District Inspector

District   Number of case

Notes

1   The provisions of section 82 apply not only to factories but also to certain electrical stations, the sites of building operations or works of engineering construction, railway running sheds, docks, wharves, quays and warehouses and certain work on ships in harbour or wet dock, ie constructing, reconstructing, repairing, refitting, painting, finishing or breaking up a ship or in scaling, scurfing or cleaning boilers (including combustion chambers and smoke boxes) in a ship, or in cleaning oil-fuel tanks or bilges in a ship or in cleaning in a ship any tank last used for oil of any description carried as cargo, and the loading, unloading or coaling of a ship in a dock, harbour, or canal.

2   A notice in this form should be given forthwith by the occupier of the factory or premises if there occurs a case of beryllium, cadmium, lead, phosphorous, manganese, arsenical, mercurial, carbon bisulphide, aniline, or chronic benzene poisoning or of toxic jaundice or toxic anaemia, compressed air illness, anthrax or epitheliomatous or chrome ulceration.

3   Notification is also required in respect of lead poisoning occurring in any other place where persons are employed in connection with the painting of buildings or in certain processes connected with the manufacture of lead or the use of lead compounds.

4   In the case of building operations, works of engineering construction, docks, work involving lead, etc the notice should be given by the employer of the person affected.

5   The notice should be sent forthwith both to the District Inspector of Factories and also to the Employment Medical Adviser for the area in which the factory is situated. Notification to the Employment Medical Adviser is not, however, required in cases of lead poisoning where persons are employed in certain processes connected with lead manufacture or involving the use of lead compounds in places other than those specified in Note 1 (above).

Printed in England
by John Corah & Sons Limited
and published by
Her Majesty's Stationery Office

3p net or
25 for 40p net (exclusive of tax)

Dd 496782 K 150 7/76
ISBN 011 881221 1

1   Occupier of factory
(or person carrying on processes at docks and certain other places)

a   Name

b   Address

c   Industry

2   Actual employer (if other than above)

a   Name

b   Address

3   Place where person affected had been working

a   Address (if different from 1b above)

b   Exact location

c   Nature of work carried on there

4   Person affected

a   Full name (surname first)

b   Sex   Age   Precise occupation (avoid the term *labourer* where possible)

c   Address

5   Nature of poisoning or disease

6   Notifications

a   Has the case been reported to the Employment Medical Adviser?

b   Has the case been reported in the General Register?

Signature of occupier, etc   Date

Figure 5:11   Weekly report of absences

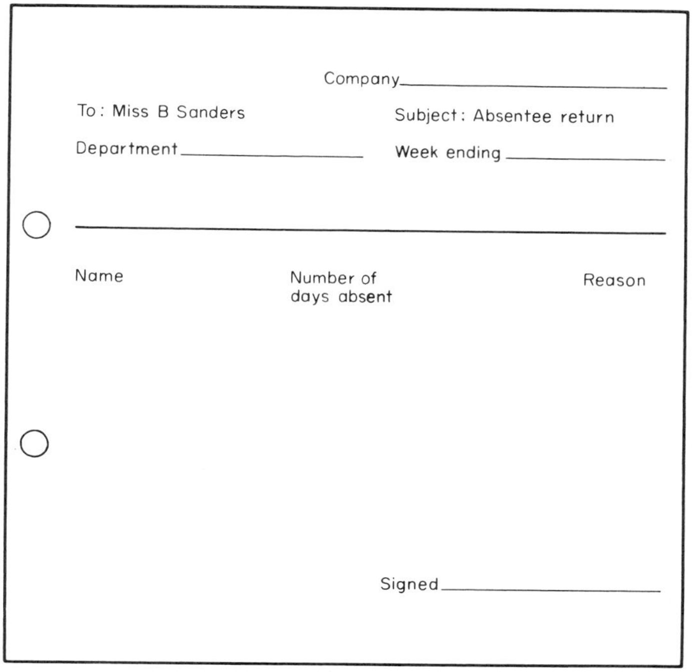

Company_____

To : Miss B Sanders   Subject : Absentee return

Department_____   Week ending _____

_____

Name   Number of   Reason
                        days absent

Signed_____

Figure 5:12   Absence record
Where any form of absence or lateness occurs, the code letter is recorded in the day's square. In the case of lateness the number of minutes is recorded (Kardex Systems (UK) Ltd)

Name (above)																								
				1972													1973							
	J	F	M	A	M	J	J	A	S	O	N	D		J	F	M	A	M	J	J	A	S	O	N	D
1													1											
2													2											
3													3											
4													4											
5													5											
6													6											
7													7											
8													8											
9													9											
10													10											
11													11											
12													12											
13													13											
14													14											
15													15											
16													16											
17													17											
18													18											
19													19											
20													20											
21													21											
22													22											
23													23											
24													24											
25													25											
26													26											
27													27											
28													28											
29													29											
30													30											
31													31											
			A			B			C							A			B			C		
			D			E			F							D			E			F		

A Illness	B Leave	C Other invalid absence	D Annual holiday
E Valid absence	F Illness or death in family		

Figure 5:13 Absenteeism record

On this record card, key information about lateness, illness, industrial injury and so on is marked in different colours. See codes next to individual's name

YEAR. 19											LATENESS, ABSENCE, HOLIDAY AND SICKNESS RECORD																						
CLOCK No.										FIGURES IN RED = MINUTES LATE A IN PENCIL = AWAITING INFORMATION II = INDUST. INJURY (RED=PAID) (BLACK=UNPAID) X C = CERT. SICKNESS(PAID) C = CERT. SICKNESS(UNPAID)									P = PERMISSION P H = PAID HOLIDAY X P = SPEC. PAID ABSENCE X U = UNCERT. SICK. BY S.P. CLAIM								E = ACCEPTED EXCUSE U = UNCERT. SICKNESS (UNPAID) C (GREEN) =1ST OR INTER. CERT. F C (GREEN) = FINAL CERT.						
NAME																																		
	BEFORE				AFTER																													
MONTH	1	2	3	4	5	6	7	8	9	10	11	12	13	14	15	16	17	18	19	20	21	22	23	24	25	26	27	28	29	30	31	REMARKS		H C
JAN																																		
FEB																																		
MAR																																		
APR																																		
MAY																																		
JUN																																		
JUL																																		
AUG																																		
SEPT																																		
OCT																																		
NOV																																		
DEC																																		

DATES WARNED FOR BAD TIME-KEEPING OR ABSENTEEISM:

Figure 5:14   Absence record

NAME														DEPT.									CHECK No.								

YEAR 19____/19____   ABSENCE RECORD

HOURS ABSENT SHOWN — { Sickness (or accident) ___ **S** *Black.*   Leave other than recognised Holidays ___ **L** *Black.*
Reasonable excuse ___ **E** *Black.* Without reasonable excuse ___*Red (Late Arrival—Red encircled — ⊕)*

MONTH	1	2	3	4	5	6	7	8	9	10	11	12	13	14	15	16	17	18	19	20	21	22	23	24	25	26	27	28	29	30	31

Dates warned for bad timekeeping or absenteeism

Over

		MONTHLY SUMMARY								A/P.L. 106—MEN

PUBLISHED BY H M STATIONERY OFFICE

MONTH	HOURS OF ABSENCE					Total Absence (incl. Late Arrival) (5)	Total Planned Hours (including overtime) (6)	% lost of Planned Hours (including overtime) (7)	No. of Occasions of Late Arrival under Col (4) (8)	Note of action taken (9)
	Sickness or Accident	Leave other than recognised Holidays (2)	With reasonable excuse (3)	Without reasonable excuse						
	Certified	Uncertified			Late Arrival	Other					
	(1)		(2)	(3)	(4)		(5)	(6)	(7)	(8)	(9)
TOTAL											

PSS04295 Wt120427 6/65 1000M J.B.Ltd. 3440 P (603)

Figure 5:15   Record of absence because of illness

This personal record is a fairly straightforward one giving permanent details of the employee as well as a record of service and seniority with the company. Illness and holiday details are recorded on the overriding sheet. The Jan–Dec scale is used to signal the month in which the yearly increment is due. The employee's occupation is signalled by a number code and the department in which he is presently employed is signalled by code letter (Kardex Systems (UK) Ltd)

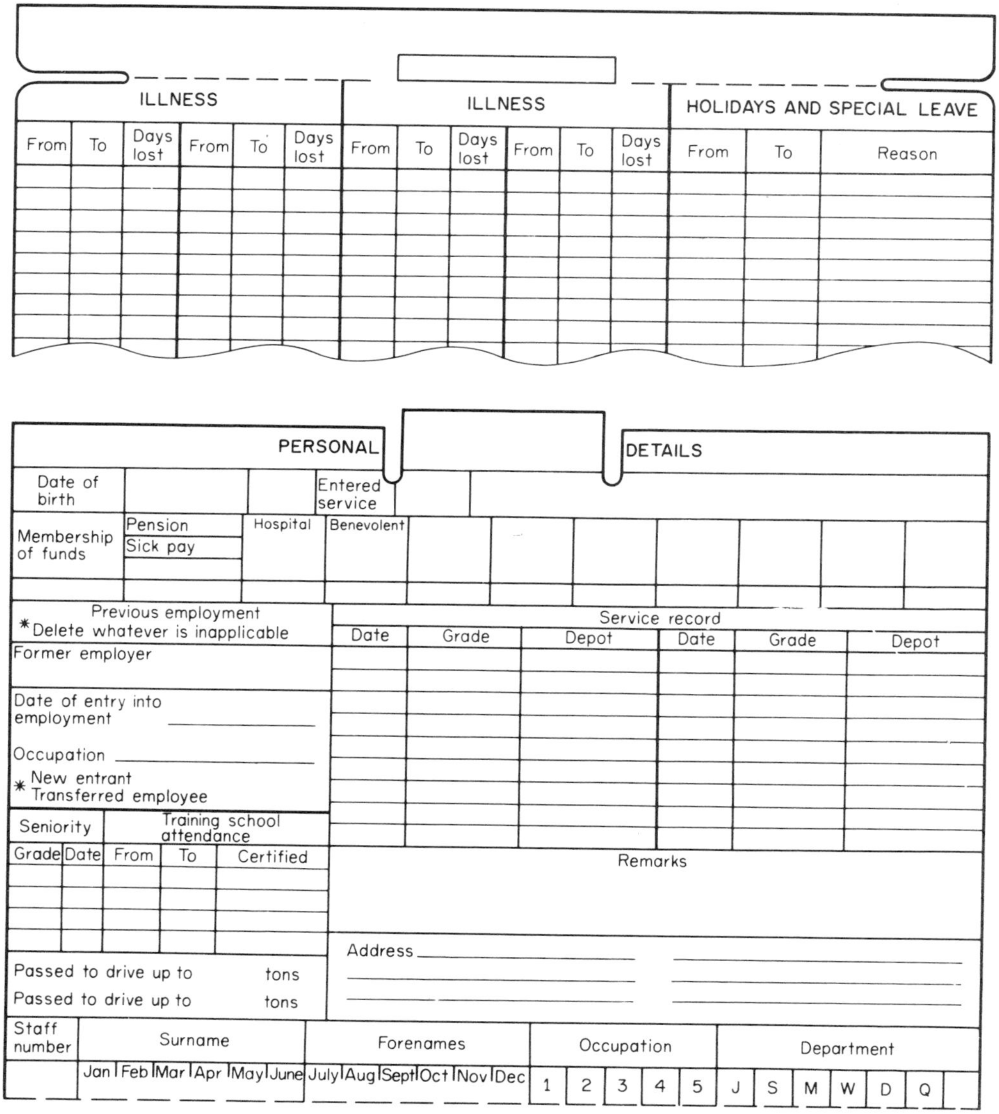

Figure 5:16 Combined personal data and attendance record

The Jan–Dec scale is used to signal the month when next wage increase is due and a lettered signal is used over the department space to signal (by code) the department in which the man is at present employed. Where a man is working on a day shift, the signal space 'shift' is left blank, but where he is engaged on a night shift a black signal is used over that space to indicate that fact

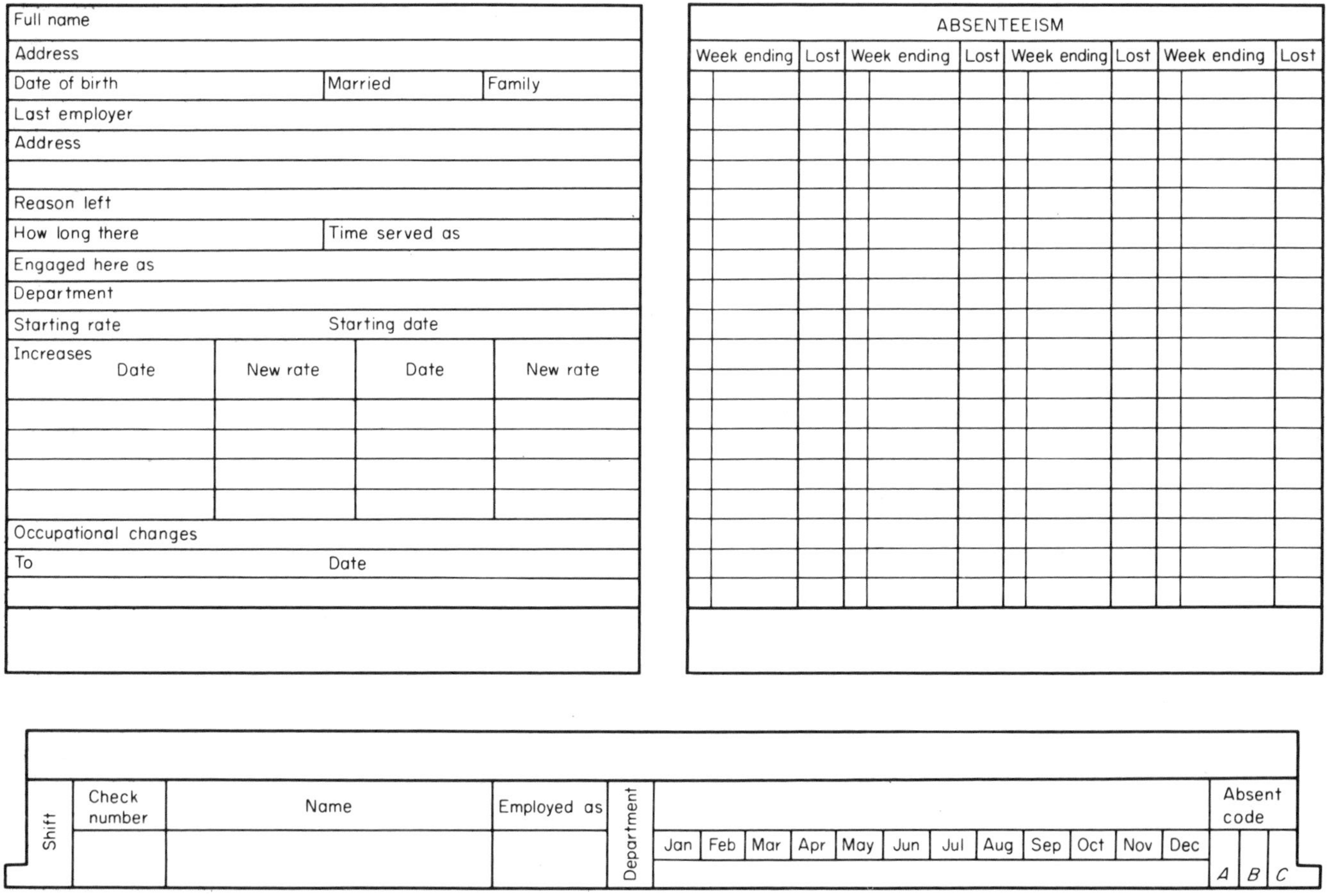

6

Training and Management Development

One of the most difficult problems for any company is to identify at an early stage those with the capacity to succeed at higher levels of management and to prepare them by training, education and experience for the responsibilities that they will have to exercise in the future. Whilst most companies now have a full-time training officer, or at least a manager responsible for training, the personnel department must remain closely involved in training as it is the department's responsibility to ensure that manpower needs are fulfilled. The department must be closely consulted regarding training needs and the actual training carried out. In most companies the personnel department is responsible for maintaining records for the purpose of the levy/exemption scheme contained in the Employment and Training Act 1973.

The Employment and Training Act modified the Industrial Training Act 1964 and provided for the Manpower Services Commission to take over many of the functions which had previously been within the ambit of training boards.

Industrial Training Board Records

The industrial training boards have made no attempt so far to impose any rules concerning the type of personnel records to be kept, although several boards provide their members with a guide and sample record cards. Figures 6:1 and 6:2 are good examples of personal training record cards with space for recording achievements. Standard training forms can be obtained from most suppliers of forms and from a number of trade and employers' associations.

Training Register

An employer wishing to qualify for a general grant or levy exemption for training carried out according to the recommendations of an industrial training board must, from the beginning of each grant year, maintain a training register of quantity and quality of training given and must be able to produce up-to-date records for the training board's inspectors as required. Training not supported in this way cannot be used for claim purposes. In general, the information in the training register should include:

1 The name of person being trained
2 The age if under 21
3 Occupation for which he or she is being trained
4 Description of the course being followed
5 The length and dates of the course
6 Details of day and block release for further education where appropriate

The Knitting Lace and Net Industry Training Board use Levy Exemption Criteria to encourage companies to operate systems which cover the following points:

– The use of job descriptions and personal specifications for selection purposes
– Employment of trained interviewers
– Use of appropriate selection documentation and record systems
– Use of selection tests where appropriate

They also require a training records system which adequately monitors the progress of trainees. The establishment of 'appropriateness or adequacy' of records is decided by a dialogue between the field training staff and the company executive responsible for training, and takes into account such factors as the size of company and the staff resources available to maintain the records system. Thus they would expect to see a greater sophistication with a large company with a professional staff than they would expect in a small company without professional expertise.

Skills Inventory

In determining long-term training needs it is useful to carry out periodic analyses of present employees with particular qualifications, professional or technical skills. Despite the obvious value of skills inventories in setting company objectives and in corporate planning, as well as establishing training programmes, few companies in fact maintain such records, primarily because of the difficulties involved. But we may see more inventories of human resources as personnel records become more and more computerised.

A skills inventory to be complete must cover everyone, including what could be called 'brainpower' resources on the professional and managerial level as well as the more technical skills and abilities. It should record the skills which are *not* available as well as those which are.

The major difficulty in compiling the necessary data from personnel records is the lack of clearly defined responsibilites for specific task and the inconsistent use of job titles. This problem has been aggravated by the growth of such activities as operational research, which require experience of employees to be re-classified in present terms.

Qualifications on record cards could include any of the following, depending on the needs of the company:

1   Physical qualifications
2   Educational qualifications
3   Technical abilities
4   Mental qualifications
5   Merit rating
6   Social data
7   Experience
8   Progress
9   Timekeeping
10 Accident record
11 Plant activities
12 Desires and ambitions
13 Education and training
14 Transfer and promotions

In addition to qualifications and achievements, it may be also feasible to indicate somehow the last type of course attended and potential courses. It is also useful to record the degree of proficiency in speaking, writing and reading a foreign language. Qualifications should be updated regularly, at the time of staff appraisal, for instance, or by reporting on a standard form qualifications achieved by individuals.

Analysis of Training Needs

To be truly effective any training given by a company must be geared to its own needs. It follows that these must be linked to company objectives, taking into consideration technological developments, market developments and marketing strategy. The recommendations of the industrial training boards should, of course, be considered, but to use them as the basis of a firm's own particular training programme is extremely unwise.

This requires a periodic and deliberate assessment of both company and, in that context, individual training needs. At shopfloor level, training needs can be identified from any of the following:

1   Accident reports
2   Reports on labour turnover, absenteeism etc
3   Consultant studies
4   Management services reports
5   Quality control records
6   Attitude surveys
7   Salary surveys
8   Amendments to procedures manuals
9   Industrial relations reports on disputes containing grievances raised in arbitration
10 Adverse probationary reports on new employees
11 Succession plans
12 Production figures
13 Reports arising from analyses of crises

Measurement of performance is perhaps the best approach to identifying individual training needs. One of the oldest, and still most useful, forms for establishing training needs of shop floor operators is the TWI Chart designed by the Ministry of Labour, now the Department of Employment, which indicates, in a simple concise form, which operator needs training, of what kind and how soon it should be achieved. This type of chart is shown in Figure 6:3.

Merit Rating

One of the most important managerial tasks of managers and supervisors is to assess employees' potential for development and promotion. They are asked to rate the employees under their supervision because they have frequent and direct contact with them and know best their qualities and shortcomings.

To ensure objectivity and fairness, many firms have some sort of merit rating procedures. Basically the objects of merit rating are:

1   To establish a standard of merit
2   To spot employees ready for promotion and/or training
3   To encourage managers to study the people under their control, to point out shortcomings which can be corrected and to give praise where it is due
4   To provide a means of determining fair rewards for merit in terms of salary increases

Many firms have a standard merit rating record which becomes an important part of an employee's file. Figure 6:4 is a typical example of a merit rating form. This record is usually compiled by the foreman, chargehand or supervisor and a copy is sent to Personnel. Sometimes a copy is returned with the signature of a personnel officer to the manager or supervisor so that he can communicate the results of the assessment to the employee at a periodic interview. Basically, this interview is to discuss his progress over the relevant period and the steps which are taken to develop the employee and improve job performance. The question of salary should not be discussed at this interview as experience shows that talking about money is not conducive to a constructive discussion. But obviously a relationship should be seen by the employee between his merit rating and wage.

In some companies the merit rating record is sent to the personnel department only after the interview, with a recommendation for training or pay increase.

Management Development

Career development within the company is essentially a matter of planning to provide experience. It calls for a constant review, at senior levels, of the management of transfers and promotions within the organisation, so that managers can be placed in jobs involving the exercise of personal responsibility which will develop and widen their capabilities.

In some companies separate records are kept for managers and others thought to be worthy of training as potential managers. These records are not elaborate. They include:

1 Personal particulars and details of education
2 Internal and external training
3 Further education courses and appointments held within the company or group, and outside if known

Performance Appraisal

At management level, training needs are best determined by some system of regular assessment of performance and potential, which would reveal individual specific strengths and weaknesses. Such an analysis would certainly consider the following areas:

1 Level of knowledge in specific subjects
2 Knowledge of specific techniques, e.g. budgetry control
3 Knowledge of company procedures, disciplinary codes, etc
4 Managerial skills such as negotiating ability, motivation of subordinates

Performance appraisal should not only help to identify training needs but also help to evaluate training already given and ensure that training programmes continue to be effective.

It was not long ago that performance appraisals attempted to assess personal qualities, such as an individual's level of initiative or how well he got on with his colleagues. With the implementation of various management by objectives programmes in British industry, however, performance appraisal has come to mean assessments of a manager's performance in terms of results against established objectives. In the light of the individual's achievements against his objectives, as agreed by himself with his superior and possibly his colleagues, specific training and other measures, such as job enlargement, job rotation, etc, can be recommended.

Details are normally filed with personal records in the personnel department and are often used in relation to periodic salary reviews and as a guide to future promotion possibilities.

There are two documents fundamental to the entire procedure of performance appraisal.

Personnel specification

The first of these two documents is the personnel specification, which is simply a list of qualifications, skills and knowledge needed to perform a job effectively.

In technical jobs requiring specific skills, it is not normally difficult to establish specifications. Managerial positions and 'knowledge' workers, however, require a bit more thought, and sometimes require analysis by behavioural scientists. Probably the best approach is to identify the attributes of people who have been proved most successful and effective in a particular job.

It should be stressed that a personnel specification is concerned with the individual holding the job and not the job itself.

This, incidentally, is the same document referred to in Chapter 2, where its use in recruitment is described. It is very rare, however, that there is an optimum fit between the successful candidate and the personnel specification, but a comparison will reveal the weaknesses of the individual.

The differences can be most easily seen graphically as shown in Figure 6:5.

In this way a personnel specification can be regarded as an invaluable training aid in identifying training needs and in constructing training programmes.

That is not to say, however, that the personnel specifications should not be modified. It is now being recognised that in practice an individual nearly always modifies his job to suit his interests, abilities and aptitudes and, equally important, may have a specific characteristic or experience which is not utilised in the original personnel specification. For this reason it is necessary to prepare individual job descriptions.

Job descriptions

The job description, as defined by the Department of Employment, is 'a broad statement of the purpose, scope, responsibilites and tasks which constitute a particular job'. A typical example of a conventional job description is shown in Figure 6:6.

The modern approach to management has extended this strict definition of a job description, however, and has given it added value in the organisation. To begin with, job descriptions in most progressive firms now include, in addition to responsibilities and tasks, the individual relationships and authority required to perform the job effectively. The kinds of headings which would be included in this more comprehensive type of job description are as follows:

1 *Title of the post* (including a general brief definition of the job)
2 *Responsible to* (to whom the job holder is accountable for his performance)
3 *Responsible for whom* (names and titles of persons reporting directly to him)
4 *Responsibilities*
5 *Authority* (limitations, if any, on the job holder's authority and limit of amount authorised for expenditure)
6 *Exceptional duties* (special and personal duties attached to the post)
7 *To liaise with* (specified by name and post)
8 *Membership of committees*

Item 4 is usually nothing more nor less than a broad statement of responsibilities and duties. These are sometimes set out under appropriate headings – for example, finance, sales, personnel. Figure 6:7 is a good example of a job description prepared as part of a management development programme.

In MBO programmes, jobs are described in terms of their output requirements – the results expected. It is argued that conventional phrases using words such as 'administers', 'plans', 'organises' and 'schedules' say nothing about what the job is intended to accomplish. The consequence is that managers tend to maintain the status quo instead of seeking improvements and innovations, which should be one of their primary tasks. Moreover, by emphasising output, greater emphasis is placed on the effectiveness of the job holder and his responsibility to contribute to organisational objectives. (See W.J. Reddin, *Effective MBO*, London: Management Publications, 1971.)

Effectiveness area

In many cases the statement of responsibilities is elaborated into a definition of effectiveness areas – that is to say, the parts of the job which are most vital to efficient performance and achieving the main objectives of the company. The idea is that managers should be encouraged to concentrate on the more productive and profitable areas and to delegate the insignificant and time-consuming tasks which otherwise tend to accumulate. It is important, therefore, in any documents used in management development programmes, to record the key results areas or effectiveness areas (the two terms are used in various types of MBO programmes) so that priority can be given to the activities where results are most vital.

The effectiveness areas provide a natural basis not only from which to monitor performance but also to identify adverse conditions and individual training needs. Against each key result area are listed the standards of performance, a description of conditions which should exist when the task is being well done, and the controls used to measure performance. The following is an example:

ESTIMATOR

To submit accurate estimates, speedily, to customers

(*a*) 90% of estimates submitted within 24 hours of receipt of query

(*b*) Errors not to exceed 1%

(*a*) Estimate control book

(*b*) Error control sheet

Figure 6:8 is a good example of a performance appraisal form. This form is, in fact, part of the document shown in Figure 6:7 and designed by the Twinlock Group. The manager writes on the 'Key results specification' form, in a distinctively coloured ink, his comments in terms of targets previously set. The old 'KR spec' as the document has come to be called within the Twinlock Group is then filed by Personnel with the new KR spec where they are made available for inspection by members of managements concerned. The remaining copies are kept by the job holder and his superior.

Although it is considered preferable to draw up a new KR spec, the old one can be amended if the revisions are minimal. Group Personnel still needs a copy of the amended KR spec, however, with the appraisal comments to avoid unnecessary administration, and so that they can be available for inspection.

At the time of submitting copies of KR specs to Group Personnel, managers are asked to outline the training to be given to the employee and to specify whether this is internal on the job, internal off the job and/or consisting of external training programmes and courses. Group Personnel advise on Group training and development policy and training needs, wherever necessary.

Group Personnel is empowered to refer to a senior manager in line authority any KR spec which appears to lack detail, objectivity, etc, although initially the matter is taken up with the manager directly concerned.

It is emphasised that Group Personnel prefers to assist the manager practically by helping him to complete the initial draft of the KR spec. After a while, with practice, a manager becomes familiar with the best method of approach and, in effect, Personnel withdraws.

The key results standards of performance and controls are also used by the Twinlock Group for the job specification which is printed on the reverse side of their standard personnel requisition form. This form, shown in Figure 6:9, is used for all personnel, incidentally, including bench hands.

Objective record sheet

Inbucon Ltd use a single document in their effective MBO programmes: an 'objective record sheet', on which is recorded each effectiveness area, the associated objective, the priority of the objective and its measurement method, the programme of activities and the actual performance achieved.

This form has many similarities to other forms used to record objectives. Its main difference is the space given to record the complete programme of activities necessary to achieve the objective. The sheet, as shown in Figure 6:10, is both a record of objectives and a useful planning document. Provision is also made for recording the actual completion date of each activity and the performance achieved towards the objectives.

This is the only document used in the effective MBO programme, as, Inbucon argue, too much paperwork causes unnecessary work for the personnel department and, worst of all, weakens the impact of the contract between a superior and his manager. Two copies of the objective record sheets are made, one for the manager and the other for his superior. The superior's superior has no copy, although he does, of course, have an objective record sheet for each of his own managers. All other paperwork support for the management development programmes – for example, measurement information – is provided by existing procedures, some of which may have been modified to serve this purpose.

Frequency

In general, there is at least one formal appraisal annually, although there are regular informal appraisals when the manager and his subordinates get together to discuss ways of overcoming the problems of the job. In some companies, performance appraisals are carried out for every manager at the same time, usually at the time of salary review. In other firms, performance appraisals are carried out in different departments at different times to avoid peaks in the clerical workload.

Within the Twinlock Group, the frequency of formal appraisals is determined by reference to the target dates in column 6 of the KR spec (Figure 6:8). If, for example, five key target dates fall between 1 April and 15 May in a particular year, the man's performance is reviewed on or about 20 May.

Training-needs Reports

In some firms, a separate document is used to record individual training needs after the performance appraisal has taken place. Figure 6:11 is a typical example of a training-needs form. This report should indicate the type of training required or recommended, and any other measures of improvement – experience in another department, for example.

In some companies the manager must decide how training gaps can best be filled and the type of training or experience required. The personnel department should give as much assistance and advice as is necessary, however, and should retain the right to make the final decision on the method most suitable.

In any case, all external management or supervisory courses should be booked through the personnel department, which will advise as necessary before making the booking. It should, for example, check that the course selected meets the particular needs and is grantworthy under the conditions of the training board.

Figure 6:1 Personal training record
This Kardex record form was designed by Kardex Systems (UK) Ltd for employees being trained. The colour signal denotes the start and/or finish of courses

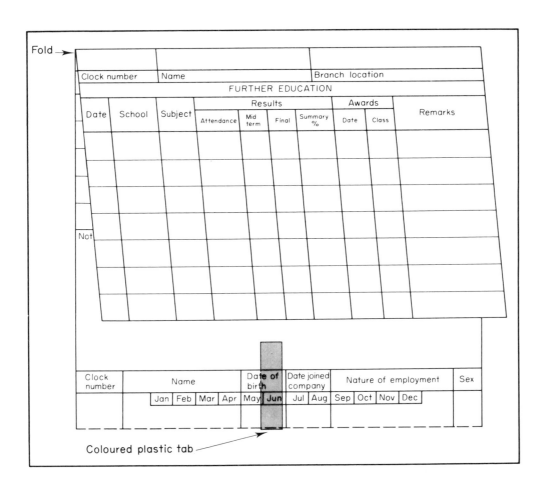

Coloured plastic tab

Figure 6:2   Personal training record

The top record is the facing card and the bottom one the main insert card. On the next page are the front and reverse of the back of the folded record card

Name of apprentice (above)

TECHNICAL CLASS RECORD

Key to grading:— A 80% − C 40% − B 60% − D below 40%	Grade	Percentage	Term	Instructed and rated by	Key to grading:— A 80% − C 40% − B 60% − D below 40%	Grade	Percentage	Term	Instructed and rated by

Parent or guardian	Commenced on As
	Commenced on As
Address of parent or guardian	Trade Pros agmt Date
School left	Indentures signed Expire Period Years Months

Interviews due

Examinations passed	With On	With On	
	With On	With On	
Languages	With On	With On	
	With On	With On	
Tendency Medium certificate	With On	With On	
National youth movement	With On	With On	

SHOP RECORD

Key to rating 1 Exceptional 2 Good 3 Average 4 Poor 5 Unsatisfactory	Ability	Interest	Speed	Accuracy	Dates From	Dates To	Rated by	Key to rating 1 Exceptional 2 Good 3 Average 4 Poor 5 Unsatisfactory	Ability	Interest	Speed	Accuracy	Dates From	Dates To	Rated by

Name (below)

Month of next transfer

Jan	Feb	Mar	Apr	May	Jun	Jul	Aug	Sep	Oct	Nov	Dec

Figure 6:2 *continued*

Apprentice transfer and shop record card	
To Mr	Department
Pupil/apprentice	Clock number
Previous shop experience	
Training in your department to be effective from	to
Training schedule to be followed	
Technical college schedule	
Will also be required to attend	
Please complete the other side and return to me when the above course is completed	
Date	
	Apprentice supervisor

To apprentice supervisor	Date
Brief details of work done	
Remarks	

RATING

	Ability	Interest	Speed	Accuracy
Exceptional	☐	☐	☐	☐
Good	☐	☐	☐	☐
Average	☐	☐	☐	☐
Poor	☐	☐	☐	☐
Unsatisfactory	☐	☐	☐	☐
Signed		Foreman		Superintendent

NOTE: As this report will form the basis of a report to the parents it is important that it be accurate.

Complaints if any against the boy can be registered under remarks. Ticks should be used in the squares

Figure 6:3 Analysis of training needs

This record of individual experience was designed along the lines of the one used in the Training Within Industry Scheme maintained by the Department of Employment. A tick against the name and under the appropriate job indicates some knowledge, a crossed tick shows sound knowledge. In this way the strength and weaknesses in the department are revealed

Department ______

Manager/Supervisor ______

Date 3-1-71 Revised 5-3-71 ; 10·9·71 ; 2-1-72

No & Name	Service: In Ind	Service: In Firm	Service: In Dpt	Other Dept	Jobs: A	B	C	D	E	F	TWI JI	TWI JR	REMARKS
J WHITE Charge Hand	14	10	8		✓×	✓×	✓×	✓×	✓×	✓×			Retires 15-9-72
S BROWN	10	5	5		✓×	✓×	✓ T/5	✓ T/4	✓	✓×			Replaces WHITE Train by 1/9
R GREEN	3	3	3		✓P T/5	✓	✓ T/5	✓×	✓×				
T BLACK	2	1	1		✓×	✓	T/5	✓	✓				On Course 8-15/2/72
M BLUE	3	2			✓P T/5		✓P T/4						Transfer if no improvement
E PINK	3				✓								Joined 1/1/72
							Move [illegible] 1/6/72		Left work 1/6/72 [illegible]				2 extra men needed for job C by 1/5/72

✓ Some exp ✓× Fully able to do the job

Figure 6:4 Merit rating record

This record is designed to be filed for future reference in a Kardex pocket file in the facing position. With each classification there is a minimum or a maximum mark (indicated by the minus or plus signs). The score for each quality is extended on the right, and the total for all qualities calculated. The total figure is shown by a graphmatic signal as indicated on the 'warnings' record illustrated in Figure 8:10 (Kardex Systems (UK) Ltd)

Name (above)	Clock number	Department	Plant	Date	Male/female	Total

	Poor − +	Fair − +	Good − +	Exceptional − +	Total
Production performance Consider the amount of work and the promptness with which completed	− 1 + 5 Unsatisfactory output	− 9 + 13 Fair output	− 17 + 21 Good output	− 25 + 29 Unusually high output	
Quality of work Consider accuracy, amount of waste and thoroughness	− 1 + 5 Major errors	− 9 + 13 Rather careless	− 17 + 21 Good quality	− 25 + 29 Highest quality	
Dependability Consider reliability and also interest, initiative and knowledge	− 0 + 2 Uncertain unreliable	− 4 + 6 Usually reliable	− 8 + 10 Trustworthy	− 12 + 14 Absolutely dependable	
Co-operativeness Consider ability to get along with other people willingness, loyalty, helpfulness, general conduct and attitude	− 0 + 2 Disagreeable and fails to co-operate, makes destructive criticism	− 4 + 6 Indifferent co-operates under pressure	− 8 + 10 Interested co-operates	− 12 + 14 Keenly interested co-operate willingly enjoys working with others	
Versatility and general knowledge Consider ability to perform jobs other than own knowledge of operations, ability to learn	− 0 + 2 One job man cannot or will not learn other jobs	− 4 + 6 Little mechanical ability learns slowly	− 8 + 10 Good mechanical ability good knowledge	− 12 + 14 Learns readily very good knowledge of other operations	Total score

Signature of foreman

Signature of supervisor

Figure 6:5   Graph comparing personnel specification with job holder's ability

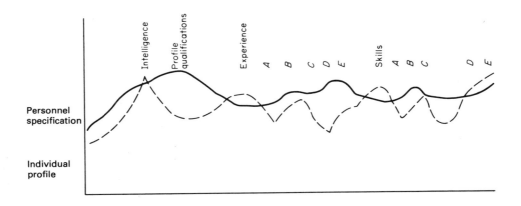

Figure 6:6 Example of a job description
Each one of the duties listed is normally subdivided into more specific tasks. Item (c)
for example might include such tasks as collating departmental sales forecasts and
drawing up production schedules and the responsibility for an adequate supply of
forecast requirements when needed

1	*Title*	Marketing services coordinator
2	*Responsible to*	Market development manager (grocery products)
3	*Positions supervised* Marketing Services Coordinator	Grocery development executive assistant
4	*Brief outline of job*	Co-ordinates and progresses all projects relating to the development of new products and packaging necessary for the growth of the department's business; provides the department with assistance relating to the development and procurement of advertising and sales promotion services

5 *Duties*

(a) Coordinates and progresses new product and packaging development projects designed to increase the grocery business of Spratt's GmbH, as well as direct export from the United Kingdom and specifically

(b) Provides the department with advice and assistance on the design and procurement of advertising and sales promotion materials and service

(c) Coordinates the production and supply of grocery products for the department

(d) Ensures that legal requirements for brand names, advertising and pack copy are satisfied

Figure 6:7 Job description

This is an example of a job description used as part of a performance appraisal form under a formal management development programme. Two copies are made out, one for the job holder and the other for personnel department files (Twinlock)

MANAGEMENT DEVELOPMENT PROGRAMME

Name _____ Grade _____   Job title _____
Company _____   Department _____

1 Purpose of job (be concise)

2 Position in organisation

Directly responsible to

Subordinates directly supervised

Working contact with

3 Resources

Personnel

Equipment

Working areas

4 Meetings and committees

5 Specific authority

Personnel

Expenditure –
              Capital
              Revenue

Other

6 Signatories

Prepared by _____ (Job holder)

Approved by _____ (Superior)

Date compiled _____ (Management analyst)

Figure 6:8 Key results specification form

This is the reverse side of the form shown in Figure 6:7 (Twinlock)

MANAGEMENT DEVELOPMENT PROGRAMME

Name of job holder_____ Job title_____ Location_____ Sheet____ of____ Date compiled____

1 Key results	2 Standards of performance	3 Controls used to measure performance	4 Degree of authority	5 Suggestions for improvement	6 Agreed action on suggestions
(ie, the main sub-divisions of the job)	(Description of conditions which should exist when the task is being well done)		(ie, full, advisory, committee)	(ie, suggestions for changes which facilitate: (a) Attainment of performance standards (b) setting of higher or more clearly defined standards (c) better controls)	(Complete with superior, detailing action to be taken and target dates. Use continuation sheets if necessary)

Figure 6:9   Job specification form (Twinlock Group)
This is the reverse side of the employee requisition form illustrated in Figure 2:2.
Only the key result areas of the jobs are listed. The second column is used to describe
the conditions which should exist when the task is being well done

Key results specification (KR spec)		
Key results	Standards of performance	Controls used to measure performance
Bench hand assemble piece parts	100	Weekly operator performance sheet

Figure 6:10 Objective record sheet

This form was designed for use in MBO programmes. A separate record is completed for each effectiveness area from which the objective derives, the precise objective, its priority, the measurement method, the programme of activities and the date when each activity should be started or completed (Inbucon Ltd)

Serials	Effectiveness area		
4	Accounting information		
4.2	**Objective** Introduce new code of accounts fully into all branches by EO July 1973	Priority **2**	
	Measurement method All branch accounts coded using new system with less than 3 errors in 1000 uncovered by monthly audit team		
	Programme of activities	**Date**	**Completed**
4.2.1	Obtain approval to introduce	EO May 71	Apr
4.2.2	Design implementation plan	EO July 72	June
4.2.3	Visit all branches to explain implementation plan	EO Aug 72	Sep
4.2.4	Conduct minimum 3 days in-tray training for all account clerks	EO Sep 72	Sep
4.2.5	Introduce in West Branch	EO Nov 72	Nov
4.2.6	Conduct 1 day seminar on West Branch introduction problem	EO Jan 72	Jan
4.2.7	Checkpoint	DUR Feb73	Feb
4.2.8	Introduce into all branches	EO Mar 73	Apr
	Actual performance Introduced new codes of accounts fully into 5 of 6 branches by EO July 1972. East Branch alone exceeded allowable 3/1000 error rate with 15/1000 error rate in August inspection. No problems anticipated in reducing this to desired level. Objective was substantially achieved		

Figure 6:11 Record of training needs

This type of form is completed by the manager after the performance appraisal has taken place

Name E Brian Ford	Job title Works Manager	Company Zenith Limited	Department Production
Manager H Goodwin		Training period: From 1-1-72	To 30-6-72

1 Was training given as planned in the previous appraisal? Yes/No
If No give reasons:
Promotion to senior position, requiring amended training programme

Date 1-12-71

2 Further training needs (Please detail and refer to section A3 in guide)

(a) Knowledge   (b) Skills   (c) Attitudes
(Detailed or appreciation)

	Category	Type	Method of training	Course title and location	GPS reference number
(a)					
(i) Detailed knowledge of production planning and control	M	Ex	SH	PERA (5 days)	
(ii) Detailed knowledge of programming work techniques including network analysis	M	Ex	SH	PERA	
(iii) Appreciation of balance sheets and profit and loss %'s	M	In-Off	S	Internal	
(b) Report-writing course (Internal?)	M	In-Off	S	Management Education Services, London	
(c) Course aimed at giving this man a better appreciation of Marketing Division problems (Internal?)	M	In-Off	S	Internal	
NOTE: J. Smith to commence Intt Works Manager course next academic year	M	Ex	DR	Inst of Works Manager – Warwick Polytechnic	

Category: M—Management: S—Supervisory: I—Instructor: C—Craft: OS—Office and sales: O—Operative: TO—Training officer

Type: Ex—External In-On—Internal on-job In-Off—Internal off-job

Method: FT—Full time: DR—Day release: BR—Block release: S—Seminar: SC—Sandwich: SH—Short course

7

Wages Administration

Wages administration is an essential part of personnel work and while its day-to-day operation may be left to the accounts department, or a separate wages department, it is ultimately the responsibility of the personnel manager to make sure that employees are paid as agreed.

Method of Payment

Wages for employees covered by the Truck Acts must be paid in current coin of the realm. This means that payment in kind or by cheque, money order or postal order is illegal without the employee's consent. Any agreement for wages to be paid in any way other than cash may be cancelled at any time by either the employer or employee who must give the other party notice in writing. Such notice takes effect at the end of the period of four weeks beginning with the day on which notice is given. An employer must pay an employee by the agreed method within a fortnight or, if he does not, at least confirm within a fortnight that he will be paying him as requested or arranged.

Employers may request their employees to sign a wages card on receipt of their weekly wages. If this system involves any appreciable delay to the employee, however, time should be allowed for them to sign during working hours to avoid delaying employees beyond the contractual finishing time.

Credit transfers

Credit transfers are a cheap and simple method for an employer to pay salaries and pensions into individual accounts. Instead of completing individual cheques to employees, the employer needs to send only one cheque to his bank to cover all payments. This system simplifies office routines, reduces stationery, accounting and administrative costs. Moreover, the employer no longer runs the risk of transporting cash to pay wages.

Where wages are to be paid into a bank account, the name and branch of the bank where the account is kept and its code number must be stated in the payroll records. Records must also indicate whether the account is in the employee's name or a joint account, in the name of husband and wife, for example.

In this system, schedules provided by banks must be completed with the payer's name, each employee's name and bank and the sums due. If the employee's bank branch sorting code number is known, only this need be given on the schedule in addition to his name and amount of transfer. Quoting individual account numbers also helps credits to be handled quickly and accurately. A suitable authority to cover payment may be incorporated in the schedule instead of writing a cheque.

The bank distributes the credit through the bank credit transfer system. Normally credits appear in the employee's accounts on the second working day after being paid in, or the third working day if paid on a Friday or Saturday. If time is too short to use the bank giro system, wages credits can be sent directly from the employer's bank to employees' bank branches.

Objections by employees to this method of payment are usually overcome by employers who are prepared to pay the basic charges of maintaining a bank account. The cost is offset against the savings on overheads and labour through the elimination of individual pay packets. The cooperation of the unions may also be obtained by arranging for members who have bank accounts to have their union subscriptions paid by standing order.

Illness

Where the employee is absent because of illness or for any other reason, payment may be made by postal or money order or by cheque, without any request or permission from the employee, unless the employed person has specifically notified the employer that he does not wish to be paid by postal order or money order when he is away. Wages sent by post, ordinary or registered, should be posted so that they will be received by the worker on the regular pay day. It would be advisable to notify workers in writing, in the employees' handbook for example, that, in these circumstances, wages will be sent to the last known address and that the onus is on them to notify the personnel or wages department of any change of adddress.

A worker who is unable to attend because of illness is entitled to authorise another person to collect the wages for him, but it is advisable to have a rule that such authority must be in writing.

Clock Cards

In order to calculate wages, many firms require the works employees, if not staff employees, to record their attendance by means of a clock card. This card bears the employee's name and a number which provides a double check on identity. This number is used on most, if not all, personnel records and a system of clock number control must be devised to prevent the same number being issued to more than one person at a time. This control may be done by the wages department but in most cases it is the responsibility of the personnel department.

Clock numbers

The system will depend on whether the clock number of an employee who leaves or is transferred can be used again for another employee within a given period – for example, the same income tax year. Some wage departments prefer that it should not be. If the clock number can be used again immediately following the departure of an employee the system will be simple: a master set of cards for all numbers or a master book register is all that is needed. If the number cannot be used again a card system is best and the cards will be in three files:

1   Available for use
2   In use
3   Out of use (until 5 April next)

The latter system, though useful in reducing the risk of error, can be inconvenient, as numbers on the clock racks must be changed fairly often if considerable gaps and extensive clock card racks are to be avoided.

Clock number control systems also act as cross-reference systems if the history cards are to be kept alphabetically. It is normally possible to discover from them who had a particular number at some time in the past.

The numbers can be used to indicate not only the department but also the sex of the person and the job or particular section where he works. This may require a five- or even six-figure number, the first two indicating the department, the next one the sex, and the last two or three the serial number within the department, possibly broken down into sections. This has the advantage of giving a good deal of quick information, but if there is likely to be much internal transfer of employees it will create a good deal of extra work for the personnel department. For this reason some firms allocate a clock number which the employee retains throughout his employment with the company no matter in which department he works.

Deductions

By law an employer is required to deduct income tax, and may deduct the employee's share of graduated National Insurance contributions. Other deductions, subject to certain limits and conditions, are allowable by statute but the employee's signature of authorisation is still required: they include:

1 Superannuation contributions
2 Retirement annuities
3 Life insurance premiums
4 Mortgage and interest payments

Other deductions which are not authorised by statute may be made, but such deductions must be voluntary and must be paid to a third party. The most common of these are for such things as:

1 Sports club
2 Sick and benevolent fund, including private health schemes
3 Pension schemes
4 Overall scheme (run by an outside body)
5 Savings scheme
6 Various charities
7 Union subscriptions

It should be noted here that the Truck Acts require the employee's signature for all deductions from the wages of manual workers that are not authorised by statute. The Truck Acts do not apply to non-manual workers, but it is not advisable for deductions to be made for any employee without his written authorisation.

It is useful to hâve a composite list of the various voluntary deductions from which an employee can strike out those he does not wish to be made before signing. This list can also be printed on the reverse side of the clock cards or job cards as a help in calculating net wages.

In the event of any of the deductions being changed it is desirable to obtain a new signature unless, as in the case of a pension scheme, the deduction follows a laid-down scheme to which the employee has agreed.

An employer may also be required to make deductions from an employee's wage under a garnishee order or under an attachment of earnings order issued by a court against an employee who owes a debt.

In cases where employers are authorised to supply their workmen with medical attendance, fuel, tools, accommodation etc, they may make deductions from wages, provided that such goods or services are supplied at cost price and that each worker concerned has given his consent in writing. An employer may not, however, deduct from an employee's pay the cost of protective clothing that the employer is compelled by law to provide.

Deductions may be made under specially stringent provisions in the law for damage caused by bad workmanship, or for any wilful damage to company property, materials and services supplied to the worker. In all instances the employee must be informed of this in writing.

Calculation of Income Tax Deductions

In order to calculate the right amount of income tax, the employer needs each employee's code number and a set of tax tables, both of which are provided by the Inland Revenue. The tax tables are designed to show the income tax due from an employee at the end of each week or month. Weekly tax tables must be used for employees paid weekly, fortnightly, or at irregular intervals. Monthly tax tables must be used for employees paid monthly, quarterly, half-yearly or yearly.

The employee's code number is shown on the monthly deduction card (P11) supplied to the employer for each employee known to be earning more than £18.50 a week or £80 per month. These cards are forwarded by the tax office before the commencement of each income tax year (6 April). The code number itself is determined by the tax office and is based on the employee's personal circumstances as reported by the employee himself on his annual tax return. Otherwise the code number is determined by the employee's annual wage, taking into account his own personal allowance.

In calculating the deduction each pay day the employer first adds to the pay due the total of all previous payments made to the employee since 6 April. The Free Pay Table (Table A) provided by the Inland Revenue shows the proportion of the employee's allowances from 6 April up to date for each code number and this figure is subtracted from the total gross pay to date. The resulting figure of taxable pay to date is then found in the appropriate Taxable Pay Table (Table B, C, BR or D) which shows the total tax due to date on any figure of taxable pay. From his figure of the total tax shown in the table the employer subtracts the figure of total tax already deducted. The remainder is the amount to be deducted from the employee's gross pay on each pay day.

Sometimes (for example, if the employee has worked a short week) the figure of total tax shown by the tax tables may be less than the tax already deducted. In that case the employer must refund the difference to the employee instead of making any deduction.

The wages earned and the deductions made for income tax must be recorded by the employer on the employee's deduction card week by week (or month by month). Space is also provided for entering the total of the employee's and employer's National Insurance contributions, the employee's contributions alone and also the amount of the employee's contribution which is calculated at the contracted out rate. If the employee receives a pension this should be distinguished from other earnings.

Returns of Income Tax Deductions

Employers are obliged to make returns to the Collector of Taxes, not later than 19 April of each year, of the pay, tax deductions and graduated National Insurance contributions in respect of all employees. This is done by sending all the deduction cards with a covering certificate (Form P35, Employer's Annual Declaration and Certificate).

On this certificate the employer is required to give the name of every employee for whom there is a deduction card, the amount of the net tax deducted or refunded and the amount of the total of the employee's and employer's National Insurance contribution, the employee's contribution and the employer's contribution at the contracted out rate (if applicable). The figures shown in each column should be added separately. If an employer finds it unduly onerous to list all the names on the form, he may, by arrangement with the Tax Office, identify the items on Form P35 by numbers, or provide a separate list.

Each deduction card must be completed to show a single figure of pay, a single figure of tax and figures of the totals of the National Insurance columns, and any other details regarding superannuation fund contributions, holiday pay, and any other payments for expenses or pay from which tax could not be deducted. An employer who does not wish to complete official deduction cards may provide two copies of a substitute document giving the same information as regards total pay, total tax and employee details. The design of the form must be approved by the tax office. The employer must undertake to keep all his payroll records for three years after the year to which they relate or longer if the Inland Revenue requires. The employer is also required by law to give to each employee at the end of the income tax year a certificate showing:

1 The total paid·by the employer to the employee during the year ending 5 April and which was taken into account for the purpose of deducting or refunding tax
2 The total net tax deducted
3 The tax code at 5 April
4 The employee's name and National Insurance number
5 Employer's name and address
6 Tax office reference

Apart from tax purposes this certificate is used by the employee for claims for earnings-related supplements to National Insurance sickness and unemployment benefits.

An official form of certificate (P60) is supplied by the Inland Revenue for this purpose. If an employer wishes to use a substitute printed form he may do so if approval is given by the Tax Office. The form must give all the information provided by the official form and the proposed design should be sent to the Tax Office for approval before printing.

National Insurance Contributions

An employer should deduct the employee's National Insurance contributions according to tables provided by the Department of Health and Social Security. Contributions are wage-related. The calculation of contributions is based on the employee's gross pay, which is normally the same as that used for calculating income tax. Contributions are related both to wage levels and also whether or not the company is contracted in or out of the State Pension Scheme.

In general, contributions must be made for all employees under the age of 65 for men and 60 for women with emoluments chargeable to income tax. Contributions are payable as follows:

Class 1 contributions, covering all employees at either of 2 rates
– contracted in
– contracted out

Full details of minimum earnings levels and percentage payable by both employer and employee are available from the Department of Health and Social Security on leaflet N.I. 208. The official deduction card, P11, provides for the entry of National Insurance contributions as well as tax deductions and is used for recording both employer's and employee's contributions.

Contributions deducted during an income tax month, together with the employer's contributions, must be paid to the Collector of Taxes within 14 days of the end of the income tax month. A single remittance can cover both payments but the remittance card (P30) must show separately the income tax and National Insurance contribution included in the remittance.

An Employer's Guide to National Insurance Contributions (Leaflet NP15) is available from the Department of Health and Social Security.

Itemised Pay Statements

Under the Employment Protection (Consolidation) Act every employee now has the right to be given a pay statement containing the following particulars:

1 The gross amount of wages or salary
2 The amounts of any variable or fixed deductions and why they are made
3 The net amount of wages or salary
4 The amount and method of payment of each part payment where these are paid in different ways

Where the deducted amounts are fixed, it is possible to give the employee a standing statement of these every twelve months. Figure 7:1 illustrates a system of pay statements which differs from the conventional ones in that it uses a vertical layout.

Payroll Summary

A payroll summary should be maintained as a record of all wages paid and deductions made. Essentially, it should show the gross pay, tax deducted, the total National Insurance contributions and any other deductions, together with cumulative totals. Figure 7:2 gives examples of payroll sheets.

In addition, the payroll summary can serve as the basic document for the analysis of labour costs, overtime or productivity measurement, for example, as well as for auditing puposes.

Earnings Records

A separate record is often kept of each employee, showing complete details of earnings, tax and insurance contributions, together with an accumulated record of earnings and tax over a period of time. This record is obviously useful in providing a complete history of an employee's earnings. Moreover, it is unnecessary, when discussing one individual, to show details of any other individual's record. Figures 7:3 and 7:4 are examples of earnings records.

The earnings record can of course be combined with the employee's personal history record in small firms where personnel and payroll records are kept together. Figure 7:5 shows an example of a personal record containing a record of earnings.

Payroll records showing the total pay, tax and National Insurance deductions for every employee must be kept for at least two years after the end of the income tax year to which the earnings relate.

An earnings record designed to suit a company's own payroll system can, with the approval of an Inspector of Taxes, be used to replace the official deduction cards required under the PAYE scheme. The basic requirement for approval is that the design conforms to the official specification (a copy of which can be obtained from any tax office) and provides the required information, as follows:

1 The whole of the identifying particulars required by the official deduction card
2 Identification of cards for pensioners and directors
3 The total of the employee's National Insurance contributions
4 Particulars of total gross pay and total tax due for the year
5 In the case of an employee leaving during the year, the date of leaving
6 Further information asked for on the deduction card – particulars of superannuation contributions, holiday pay and so on

Where only annual totals are shown, employers must incorporate the necessary figures of pay and National Insurance contributions in their pay records over the income tax year, supply two copies of their documents at the end of the year and also undertake to keep their pay records for at least three years after the end of the year.

Integrated Payroll Systems

There are various integrated payroll systems designed to provide entries on each record at one writing. Generally the payroll summary is placed on top of a sheet of pay slips and each earnings record placed over the payroll sheet in turn for simultaneous recording of entries. The payroll summary sheet is then totalled to give the total wages.

Figure 7:6 shows a type of multi-posting payroll system. The payroll statements in the system are in perforated sheets. A second system, shown in Figure 7:7, is in fact used for preparing vertical statements. The statements are overlapped with runs of up to eighteen so that each right-hand column is exposed. The figures are then added across to obtain the cumulative total of the full payroll. The payroll summary sheet has space for twenty-six weeks of each earnings record.

Standard payroll sheets, earnings cards and pay statements are available in a variety of formats for various purposes. But in each case, the format of the payroll documents used together must be the same for simultaneous completion of entries. Figure 7:2 shows two different formats for payroll summaries and statements each with its own distinctive features. The first is a general layout providing for date, hours and rate at the beginning, basic pay plus bonus, commission, normal statutory tax calculations columns for such things as holiday and sickness payments schemes. The other is similar except that it provides on the right-hand side in addition to the net pay a column for non-taxable allowances. This is useful where non-taxable allowances are paid with salary, such as a flat-rate car depreciation allowance.

Schedule of Wage Rates

It is also common practice for the personnel department to hold a schedule of wage rates and salary grades giving an accurate picture of the rate for every job, including any range of rates and maximum bonus applicable to the job.

Although it is for senior management to negotiate and fix the terms of employment it is the personnel department's task to implement the schedule and to modify it as data are received from annual performance review or when new agreements are made between trade unions and management. It is the personnel manager's responsibility to note any anomalies in the wage structure and wage drifts to ensure payroll costs do not exceed budget forecasts.

A typical wage structure has for each grade a basic pay or rate which, theoretically at least, represents the relative worth of the job to the company. The basic wage for the various grades is best determined by using job evaluation techniques, particularly in situations where there are many types of jobs.

There will normally be a number of other elements to recognise personal performance, such as productivity bonuses, overtime premiums, shift premiums, etc, age and/or service and, sometimes, additional payments to cover dirty or dangerous conditions and extraordinary weather conditions. In addition there may be special proficiency rates, training allowances, temporary transfer rates, special rates for part-time workers, first-aiders, etc, holiday pay and redundancy pay. Many of these extra payments can be incorporated into the basic rate much more frequently than usually occurs in practice, however.

It may often be necessary to trace the history of the rate for the job and it is important therefore to retain copies of earlier schedules showing exactly when they were operative. Sometimes a history of the rate for each job may be kept, or a record of average wages for different jobs, though this record is more commonly maintained by the wages department.

Labour Cost Records

As it is the responsibility of the personnel department to uphold the wage schedule, continuous administration is necessary to ensure that labour costs do not go out of line.

There should be close consultation between the personnel department and senior managers concerning the amount of salary increases before performance appraisals to ensure that recommended salaries do not conflict with company policy. Personnel should subsequently analyse the increases awarded for anomalous marks, possible departmental bias and unjustified changes in assessment. All unusual changes in salary or assessment should be automatically brought to the notice of the personnel manager.

Below supervisory level, labour cost control is a bit more difficult. The only sensible way of getting the information required is by carrying out regular analyses of the pattern of wage trends, including all payment above the basic rate. For a detailed analysis of wage and earnings, the following information is required for each employee under review over an appropriate reference period:

1 Job number or code
2 Basic rate or grade rate per hour
3 Gross average earned rate per hour/week
4 Forty-hour average earned rate per hour/week
5 Average overtime premium
6 Average shift premium
7 Average hours a week
8 Range of earnings (to show fluctuations)

In most companies this information can be collated from wages cards. Obviously the only sensible way of making sure that the desired information will be available as required is by involving Personnel or at least making Personnel interests known from the start when designing payroll systems.

With incentive schemes it may be feasible to have employees record lost time of more than, say, ten minutes. This will mean that regardless of the supervision, a man's time can be accurately recorded. Figure 7:8 shows a simple clock card for recording on and off time. If clocking on and off lost time is not acceptable, a card can be kept in the foreman's office for each man on which entries can be made by the foreman. Some disagreement can obviously arise when a foreman cannot be found, however, and this could provide a loophole in any incentive scheme.

Details of the causes of lost time, which should be recorded, are valuable in the interests of improving productivity. Codes can be used to indicate the category of lost time:

1 Waiting equipment
2 Waiting instruction
3 Machine not available
4 Waiting for other trades
5 Waiting work
6 Discussions with supervision
7 Union trouble or business
8 Medical room

Wage and Salary Analyses

The personnel department may be called upon to provide data necessary for negotiations or for developing new wage structures and payment methods. For this reason it is important that wage records are not only comprehensive and accurate but are in a format which enables quick and simple analyses to be carried out. In addition to the distribution of current earnings, management negotiators and union representatives may seek information on the past growth of earnings, for example. This can be provided by plotting the average hourly rate over a period of years against an index value. It is also useful to include the average performance level against a similar index scale over the same years. If this can be done from the information available, the extent that wages have moved relative to productivity can be clearly displayed.

It is also useful to keep a record of all overtime hours worked by department or section and possibly for each employee, indicating the number of hours and the number of days worked overtime. Clock cards can be arranged for the direct punching of information from the card for computer calculation. The calculation of total clock hours, and hours on each class of overtime, can be performed by hand in the wages office and written on the card. The required information can be put onto punched cards for ease of analysis.

Where payroll calculations are computerised, this information and control data, such as grade scales, can be easily programmed.

Figure 7:1   **Example of vertical pay statement** (Kalamazoo)

PAY ADVICE

Kalamazoo
BUSINESS SYSTEMS
18203-11½x3

	Week or Month No.	Date	1	9/4
	Details			
Earnings	A		60	~
	B		10	–
	C		5	–
	D			
	E			
	Gross Pay		**75**	**–**
Superannuation				
Gross Pay for Tax Purposes			**75**	**–**
Gross Pay to Date for Tax Purposes			75	–
Tax Free Pay			24	80
Taxable Pay to Date			50	20
Tax Due to Date			17	50
Tax Refund				
Deductions	Tax		17	50
	* N.I. Contribution (Employee)		4	31
	0			
	1			
	2			
	3			
	4			
	5			
	6			
	Total Deductions		**21**	**81**
Net Pay			53	19
F				
G				
Total Amount Payable			**53**	**19**
N.I. Contribution (Employer)				
N.I. Total (Employer & Employee)			12	37
H				
* Contracted-out Contribution included above				

YOUR PAY IS
MADE UP AS
SHOWN ABOVE

Miller
K.E.

Figure 7:2 Payroll sheets (George Anson Ltd)

PAY ROLL

SHEET No. ____________

WEEK/MONTH ENDING ____________

DATE	HRS. RATES Etc.	EARNINGS								INCOME TAX				NAT. INS'CE CONT'NS			OTHER DEDUCTIONS					
		BASIC	A	B	C	GROSS PAY FOR WEEK/MONTH	LESS: SUPERANNUATION	NET PAY FOR WEEK/MONTH	ACCUMULATIVE NET PAY TO DATE	TAX FREE PAY	TAXABLE PAY TO DATE	TAX DUE TO DATE	INCOME TAX REFUND	TOTAL OF EMPL'ERS + EMPL'EES CONT'NS	EMPL'EES BASIC CONT'N		1	2	3	TOTAL DEDUCTIONS	AMOUNT PAYABLE	NAME

PAY ROLL

SHEET No. ____________

WEEK/MONTH ENDING ____________

DATE	EARNINGS							INCOME TAX				NAT. INS'CE CONT'NS			OTHER DEDUCTIONS							
	BASIC	A	B	GROSS PAY FOR WEEK/MONTH	LESS: SUPERANNUATION	NET PAY FOR WEEK/MONTH	ACCUMULATIVE NET PAY TO DATE	TAX FREE PAY	TAXABLE PAY TO DATE	TAX DUE TO DATE	INCOME TAX REFUND	TOTAL OF EMPL'ERS + EMPL'EES CONT'NS	EMPL'EES BASIC CONT'N		1	2	3	TOTAL DEDUCTIONS	PAY LESS DEDUCTIONS	ADD: NON-TAXABLE ALL'CES	AMOUNT PAYABLE	NAME

Figure 7:3 Earnings record (George Anson Ltd)

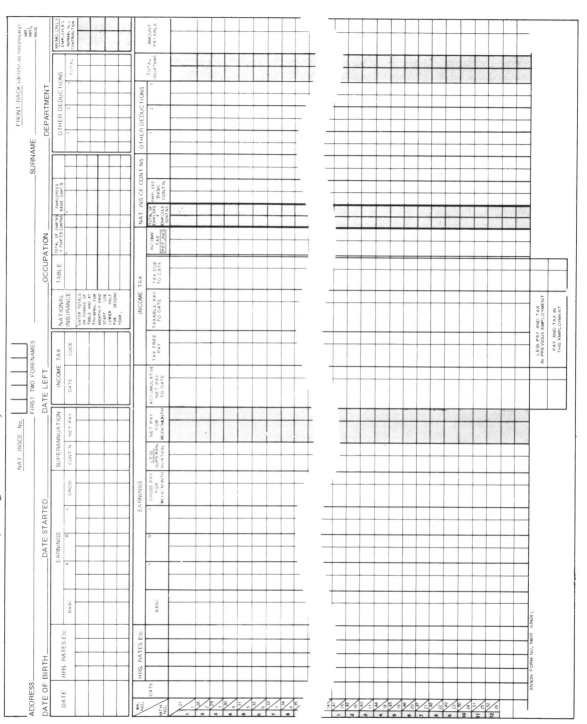

Figure 7:4 Earnings record (Moore Paragon UK Limited)

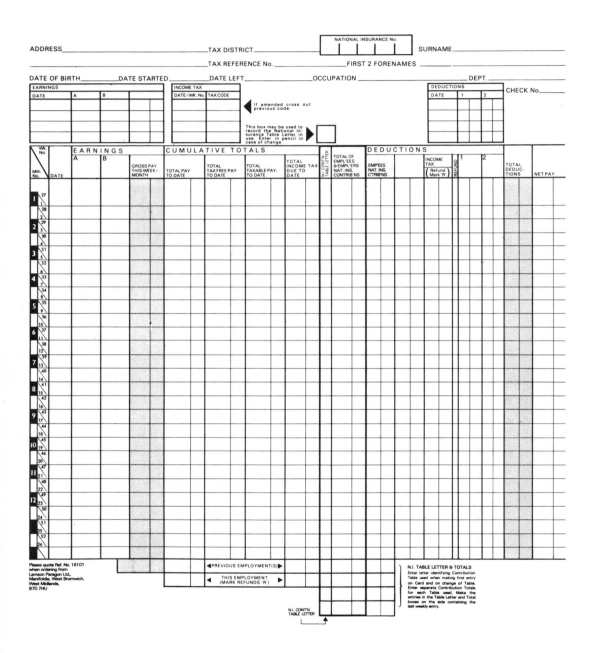

Figure 7:5 Personal record containing a record of earnings

Surname		Forenames		Company		Depot	

Department		Present job			Clock number	

Address		Phone number

Change of address		Phone number

Marital status	Next of kin	Address

Date of birth	Nationality	Registered disabled

Engaged as	Transfer

Date of engagement	National Insurance number

Previous employer

Job	Period of employment

Previous 600 group experience	Job	Reason for leaving

Remarks

WAGE RECORD

Department	Job	Rate	Date and reason for change	Department	Job	Date	Date and reason for change

Name	Clock number	Job	Department	Company	Depot

Figure 7:6   Multi-posting payroll system for bank giro payments (Anson Systems Division of OCÉ Skycopy BV)

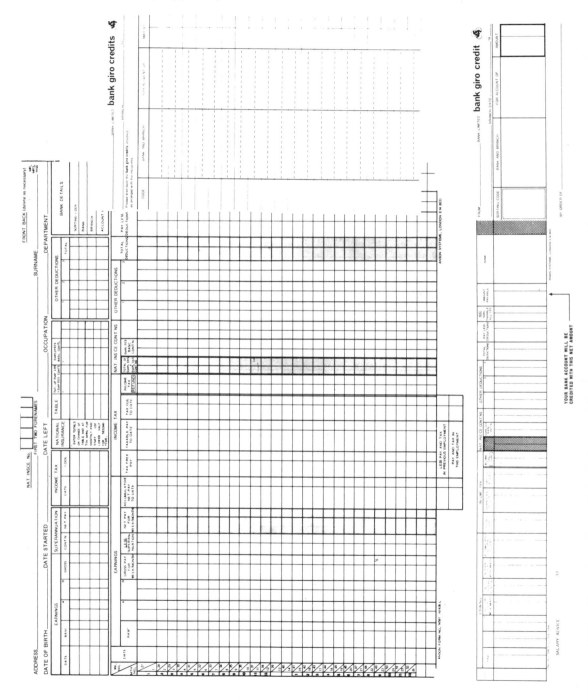

Figure 7:7 Integrated payroll system (Kalamazoo)

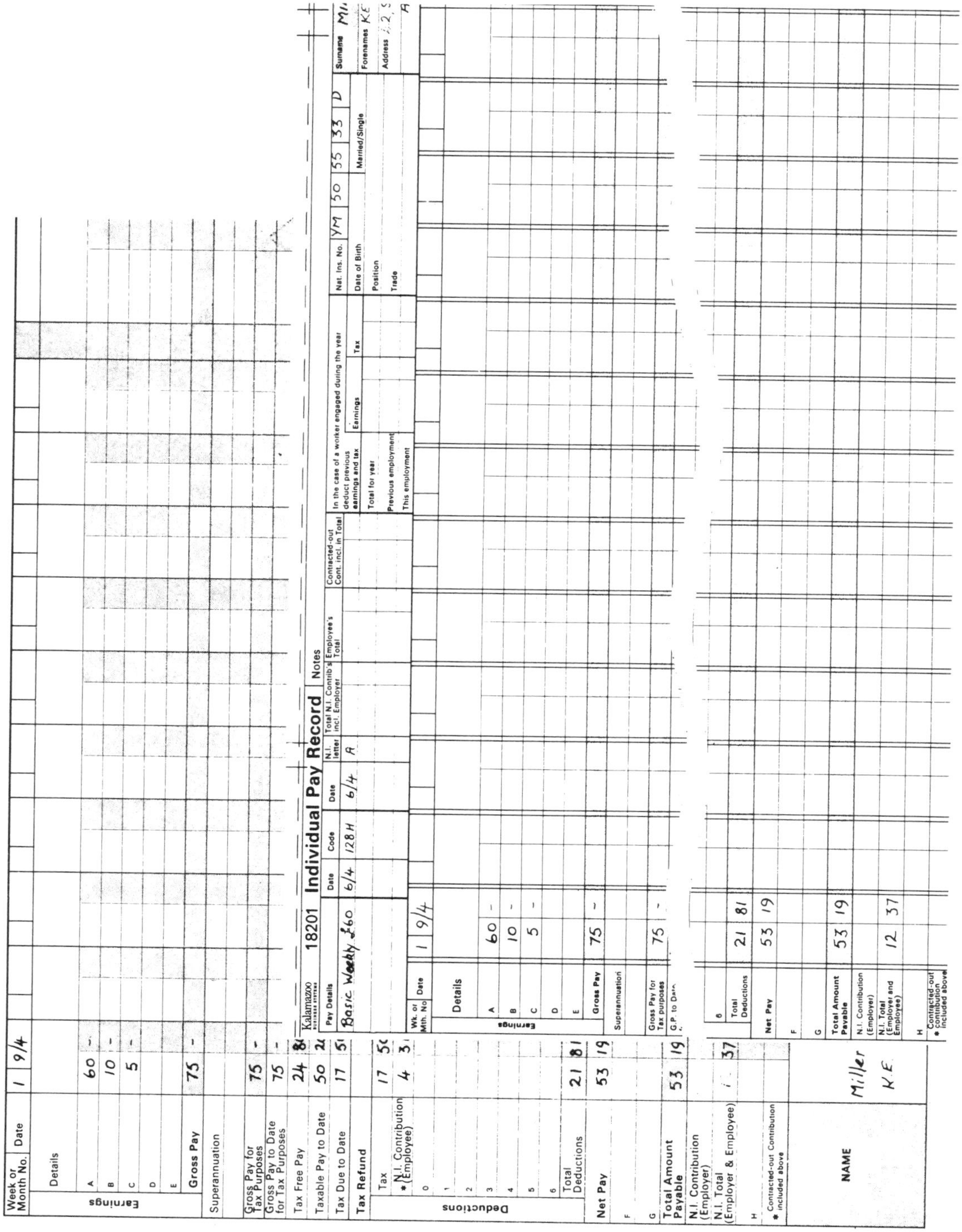

Figure 7:8   Lost time card

	On	Category	
	Off		
	On		
	Off		
	On		
Name_____	Off		
	On		
Clock number_____	Off		
	On		
	Off		
	On		
	Off		
	On		
	Off		
	On		
	Off		
	On		
	Off		
	On		
	Off		
	On		
	Off		
	On		
	Off		
	On		
	Off		
	On		
	Off		
	On		
	Off		
	On		
	Off		
	On		

8

Termination of Employment

The Employment Protection (Consolidation) Act gives all employees, employed continuously for four weeks or more, the right to minimum periods of notice, and it is becoming increasingly important for the personnel department to be notified immediately of any pending termination (a central co-ordination of dismissal standards and procedures helps to reduce the possibility of claims for unfair dismissal).

An employer is required to give:

- one week's notice to an employee employed for more than four weeks and less than two years.
- at least two weeks' notice if the employee has been employed for two years or more.
- one additional week's notice for each further year of employment up to a maximum of twelve weeks if the employee has been employed for twelve years or more.

The employee is only required to give one week's notice after four weeks' employment and it does not increase with longer service. However, these requirements are minimum standards and do not preclude contracts from requiring longer periods, both from employer and employee.

Most firms require notice to be given in writing and there is now a legal requirement under the Employment Protection (Consolidation) Act that the employee must be provided by his employer, on request and within fourteen days, with a written statement giving particulars of the reasons for his dismissal. This statement is admissible in evidence in any proceedings and refusal to provide it will result in a tribunal making an award that the employer pay the employee a sum equal to the amount of two weeks' pay.

Legislation covering unfair dismissals, trade union membership (Trade Union & Labour Relations Act), maternity provisions (Employment Protection (Consolidation) Act, racial discrimination (Race Relations Acts), sex discrimination (Sex

Discrimination Act) and ex-offenders (Rehabilitation of Offenders Act) has meant that records covering termination have achieved considerable importance.

Termination Forms

Termination by the employee is normally recorded on a form by the supervisor and sent to the personnel department for action. It generally carries the name and clock number of the employee, the effective date of termination, reason for leaving and sometimes comments on whether or not the employee is suitable for re-engagement.

However, some firms prefer to record confidential statements of opinion on a separate form.

Figures 8:1 and 8:2 show examples of forms used to notify termination. A duplicate copy of a termination advice may go directly to the wages department or personnel department will inform wages department possibly by raising a wages clearance or release form which includes a checklist showing that the employee has been cleared by stores for borrowed equipment or clothing (see Figure 8:3).

Termination by the employer is usually a result of

– a requirement for fewer employees (redundancy)
– alleged failure of the employee to observe certain standards of conduct at work or to achieve certain levels of job requirements (dismissal)

When an employee leaves the company, the employer must prepare a form P45 (certificate 'Particulars of Employee Leaving', shown in Figure 8:4) showing the total earnings in the current income tax year to the date of leaving and the total amount of tax which has been deducted.

Part 1 of the form is sent by the employer immediately to the Inspector of Taxes and parts 2 and 3 are handed to the departing employee who may also be given a blank form P50, if it is known that he is not taking up new employment. Form P50 is required by the employee to claim any refund of tax which may be due to him should he become temporarily or permanently unemployed. If the employee has died, a *D* is entered in a box indicated on the form and all three parts are sent to the tax office.

In the case of an employee still affected by a garnishee order or an attachment of earnings order who ceases employment for any reason, the employer must notify the appropriate officer of the court that made the order.

Redundancy

When employment is terminated because of redundancy the employer is obligated to make a redundancy payment to employees who qualify. To qualify for a redundancy payment an employee must have worked for sixteen hours or more a week, have completed a minimum of 104 weeks' continuous service with the present employer, and be between the ages of eighteen and sixty-five (or sixty for women).

Redundancy payments

According to the Employment Protection (Consolidation) Act, the redundancy payment must be made immediately upon termination of employment, the amount dependent upon age and years of service, as follows:

1 For each complete year of service (maximum twenty years)
   after forty-first birthday $1\frac{1}{2}$ weeks' pay
2 For each complete year of service, apart from those covered by
   1 after twenty-second birthday 1 week's pay
3 For each complete year's service apart from those covered by
   1 and 2 after eighteenth birthday $\frac{1}{2}$ week's pay

Reckonable service is limited to the twenty years prior to redundancy. Calculation of a week's pay for all employees is defined in the Employment Protection (Consolidation) Act. Payments are calculated on a maximum wage of £110 a week. Any earnings above this amount are not taken into account. The maximum payment under the scheme is therefore £3,300.

Ideally, redundancy payments should be given separately from regular wage payments, and handed individually to the employee as a manifestation of the company's concern.

Employment protection legislation now provides a procedure for handling redundancies and certain redundancies need to be notified to the Secretary of State on Form HR1. This form or a letter containing full particulars, i.e.:

- reasons
- numbers and description of redundant employees
- total number of people employed
- method of selection for redundancy
- proposed method of carrying out dismissal
- collective agreement, if applicable
- trade unions involved
- date consultation began

should be sent to the Regional Office of the Department of Employment.

Employees have more job security now that employers are required to consult appropriate trade unions whenever they propose to make even a single employee redundant.

Full details of the Redundancy Payments Scheme and the forms available can be obtained from the redundancy payments office of the Department of Employment or the Employment Service Agency.

Rebate claim

The employer may claim a rebate for redundancy payments, from a fund to which he has contributed, no later than six months after the date of termination of the employment, unless the matter has been referred to a tribunal within this period. Form RP3 shown in Figure 8:5 must be completed and sent to the local Department of Employment office unless the redundancy payment is being reduced because of pension in which case form RP3 (Pen) should be used.

The claim must be made in writing and must include the date on which the employment terminated and the method by which the amount of the employer's payment has been calculated. Form RP2, shown in Figure 8:6, must be used for claiming rebate from the redundancy fund. Notice must be given not less than fourteen days before the date on which the termination of employment is, or is expected, to take effect. Where the contracts of ten or more employees are to terminate on the same day or within a period of six days, prior notice of at least twenty-one days is required by law. Form RP1 shown in Figure 8:7 should then be sent to the local office of the Department of Employment.

If it is not practicable to give all the information required in the notices then they should be delivered before the time-limits but with a note that some information will follow. The missing information must be delivered as soon as practicable to the same local office as that to which the notice was delivered. If any of the required information is not known or not completely known to the employer, that fact must be stated.

Offer of alternative work

If an employee unreasonably refuses an offer, either of a renewal of his contract of employment to take effect immediately or of suitable alternative employment, either with the same firm or with a subsidiary or parent company, he is not entitled to a redundancy payment. The offer must be made to the employee before the due date of termination of the job and the alternative employment must start within four weeks.

The offer must be in writing. It should contain enough particulars to give a clear idea of what is being offered – what the work is, where it is, rates of pay and any other terms and conditions that are different from those under which the employee has been working up to then. Figure 8:8 gives an example of a form for use as a written statement offering redundant employees alternative work. These signed statements should be filed with the employee's personal records to protect the employer from any future claim for redundancy pay. An employee who accepts an offer of alternative employment is allowed a trial period to find out if the job is really suitable for him, without losing his right to redundancy payment.

Dismissal

The Employment Protection (Consolidation) Act makes it unwise for an employer to dismiss an individual without a just and fair reason. Where the employee claims he has been unfairly dismissed it is for the employer to show that the reason for dismissal was fair or pay compensation.

The interpretation of the provisions of the Act regarding unfair dismissal is likely to be contentious. In practice, dismissal on grounds of the employee's capability, qualifications, conduct or for other substantial causes will be considered reasonable grounds for dismissal. These reasons will, however, hardly be sufficient in the case of long-service employees who have no previous record of substandard performance or misbehaviour.

Before an employee is dismissed for any reason, adequate warnings should be given and these recorded to establish that they were given. In certain circumstances it will be of considerable importance to state whether an employee has been warned about committing breaches of the rules, for slackness, lateness, etc. Broadly speaking, these misdemeanours fall under the following headings:

1   Defective work   4   Absence
2   Misconduct   5   Disobedience
3   Lateness   6   Carelessness

Whatever the reason for dismissal, the personnel department should be fully involved before it takes place so that the possibility of retraining or transfer to a more suitable job can be considered.

Notice

There is no common practice in the length of notice to be given by employees, but the majority are content to give only the minimum required by law. Under the Employment Protection (Consolidation) Act an employer is required to give an employee:

1   At least one week's notice if the employee has been with him continuously for four weeks or more
2   At least two weeks' notice if the employee has been with him continuously for two years or more
3   Thereafter one additional week's notice for each year of service, up to a maximum of twelve weeks.

In order to provide a guide to dealing with dismissals the Advisory, Conciliation and Arbitration Service issued a Code of Practice covering disciplinary procedures in employment. This in turn has identified the need for certain forms which might eventually lead to termination procedure.

Figure 8:9 shows an example of a written warning. Figure 8:10 shows an example of a record of warnings.

Maternity Rights

The Employment Protection (Consolidation) Act gives three important new rights to a woman who is expecting a baby:

1 The right not to lose her job – pregnancy itself will not be a valid reason for dismissal
2 The right to return to her job after the baby is born
3 The right to maternity pay

The first depends upon the woman having worked for her employer for at least 26 weeks. To obtain the other two rights she must have worked for her employer for at least two years by the eleventh week prior to her confinement.

If the woman, subject to certain conditions, wishes to return to work after the baby is born, it is wise for the company to ascertain this fact at the exit interview (see page 171), although at this stage the woman may not be sure in her own mind. Records need to be kept of the actual date she finished work, the expected date of confinement, the actual date of the birth of the baby and there should be written confirmation of either *a*) her final termination or *b*) her expressed wish to return to work.

Maternity pay, again subject to certain conditions, is payable for the first six weeks and employers who have made maternity payments are able to claim back the full amount, up to the limit that the Act requires them to pay.

Full information about this section of the Act is available from the Regional Offices of the Advisory, Conciliation and Arbitration Service or the local offices of the Department of Employment.

Figure 8:11 shows Form MP1 which allows for claim of rebate of maternity pay. Figure 8:12 is the employee's receipt for maternity pay [MP1 (R)].

Labour Turnover Analysis

The real reasons for employees leaving are never easy to determine, but they are necessary if an employer is interested in reducing the rate of labour turnover. Some turnover is fortuitous, of course, and on occasion may be desirable. The main objective of Personnel is to control turnover where it is avoidable and is most damaging. This requires an anlysis of the reasons for particular individuals leaving.

A basic list of the reasons for leaving is often printed on the reverse side of a termination form or a personal history card, such as the one shown in Figure 8:2. In this way the reason can simply be ticked or a code used to make completion of the form that much easier. This ensures a consistent use of terms and avoids the use of several terms for the same reason, thus facilitating the compilation of statistics. The list below is a good basis for such a list:

1	Remuneration	10	Transport difficulties
2	Nature of work	11	Housing difficulties
3	Hours of work (shift or non-shift)	12	Move from district
		13	Domestic responsibilities
4	Physical working conditions	14	Illness
5	Dissatisfaction with job	15	Accident
6	Dissatisfaction with supervisor	16	Marriage
7	Dissatisfaction with other workers	17	Pregnancy
		18	Age
8	Lack of opportunities	19	Retirement
9	Personal betterment (which could include pay)	20	Death
		21	Discharged

The last factor may be subdivided into:

1 Unsuitable
2 Disciplinary reasons
3 Redundancy

It has been suggested that factors can be conveniently classified under the following headings:

1 Outside economic factors which affect the labour market and which impinge on the work situation, such as the level of employment
2 Factors within the employing organisation which affect the employee
3 Factors within the employee as an individual, or within groups of employees

The Industrial Society recommends that reasons for leaving can be more conveniently classified as controllable, uncontrollable and discharge, as only controllable factors are of any value for the purposes of personnel research and analysis.

Exit interviews

Although exit interviews are acknowledged to be inadequate they are still the prime source of information and are still depended upon by a large number of companies. To get the most out of them requires great preparation and imagination. To begin with, the employee may not be prepared or able to give his reasons precisely. In some instances it may be unlikely that he would give his true reason to his immediate supervisor who himself may be the cause. Line managers may not be sufficiently skilled in interviewing to differentiate between the real reason and the straw that broke the camel's back.

Even where properly conducted exit interviews are held it is very difficult to establish the real reason for leaving. In fact few people leave for one single reason. There may be several underlying dissatisfactions which the employee has felt for some time before something precipitates his leaving. These dissatisfactions may be forgotten or concealed at an interview. Exit interviews are more useful if considered as a survey of attitudes rather than as providing accurate reasons for leaving.

Some companies arrange two interviews, one with the man's immediate supervisor and the second with *his* superior, so that, hopefully, the real reason may be determined by combining both replies. In particularly bad situations it may be feasible to arrange interviews with a senior manager, whom the leaver knows is in a position to rectify a problem situation, or to retain a third party, possibly a psychologist or management consultant who is experienced in eliciting truthful responses and summarising attitudes.

If it is felt that an unnecessary amount of manager's time is being expended in exit interviews, it should be remembered that the same, if not more, time can be spent in interviewing new recruits. It is, however, usually neither possible nor profitable to interview everyone who leaves a company. It may not be worth interviewing young girls, even in sections with a high rate of labour turnover, for whom getting a new job is very much like buying a new dress. One should concentrate on managerial and specialist grades and other key personnel.

Interview forms

The results of interviews are sometimes stated on standard forms which are signed by the interviewer and a personnel officer and used for statistical purposes. One large company uses such a form which is divided into a number of parts. The first part is completed for all leavers. It consists of a standard classification of reasons for leaving, from language difficulty to 'head-hunted', personal details, date of engagement, job specification and future employment. Further comments have to be made on additional parts for those leaving with more than ten years' service, those who were dismissed or asked to resign, technicians, apprentices, graduate trainees or direct entry graduates. In the case of graduates, the termination forms are seen and signed by the managing director as well as the personnel manager.

Others use a termination interview form (Figure 8:13) which is completed by both the employing department and Personnel and which stresses the leaver's attitude to the company.

Besides conducting exit interviews, a few companies check their recruiting procedures by sending questionnaires to former employees several weeks or even months after their departure. The belief is that the former employee is spared the embarrassment of a face-to-face confrontation with a senior manager and has time to see his own reasons for leaving in a clearer perspective. Results of experiments with post-departure surveys show great differences in answers given by the same people at exit interviews. Philips Industries once found that 57 per cent of leavers questioned a year after they had left gave a totally different reason from the one given at the time of leaving.

It may be useful to interview not only those leaving but also remaining employees. To prevent the rate of turnover increasing requires a regular audit of the state of morale within each department, the use made of employees and an investigation of possible conflicts of personalities and even the manager's managerial deficiencies. This can be done as part of a broader attitude survey which not only helps to give an indication of the likely acceptability of a course of action, but can be a very useful exercise in participation.

Labour turnover statistics

A statistical breakdown of labour turnover is essential for identifying the cause of the problem which in turn enables a company to take the necessary steps to reduce the problem and its effects. Regular analyses of labour turnover will indicate weaknesses in personnel policy or practices. They can identify problem areas in, for example, the wage structure or recruitment procedures. This is important, as when a person leaves, or even if he is sacked, it is often recruitment that has failed, not the employee.

Labour turnover – the number of people joining and leaving a company or department – is normally measured according to the percentage of the total work-force who have left in a particular period. Statistically this is represented as:

$$\frac{\text{people left}}{\text{people in workforce}} \times 100\% \text{ per month/year}$$

For example, if in one month a department lost four people from a total of 20; labour turnover would be:

$$\frac{4}{20} \times 100\% \text{ per month} = 20\% \text{ per month}$$

Statistical reports

In most companies labour turnover statistics are collated annually and, with a report on the causes, circulated among senior management. Results are usually unremarkable and merit little attention outside Personnel.

Within Personnel, analyses of labour turnover are given careful consideration and, in an increasing number of companies, are looked at on a monthly basis, instead of annually, as a sort of early warning system. Figure 8:14 shows a monthly report used for analysing labour turnover.

Very often companies use interdepartmental comparisons as a spur to individual managers to pay attention to the problem of turnover. Labour turnover figures are made available to managers each month so that they may compare their department's figures with others and with the company as a whole. If labour turnover is high, it is the manager's responsibility to pinpoint the cause and effect, and take remedial steps, although Personnel Department may give any help necessary.

Labour turnover statistics need to be broken down into greater detail, however. A cursory examination of the turnover rate may lead a company to conclude that it has or has not an excessive wastage compared to similar organisations – but the company records may not be sufficiently detailed to draw any such conclusions. It is necessary to have a statistical breakdown of leavers in order to reveal the source of trouble.

Whilst the total rate of labour turnover may be considered satisfactory, greater analysis may reveal unsatisfactory areas. A high turnover among unskilled and semi-skilled workers, for example, may indicate a need for more careful placement, in accordance with intelligence, and the need for testing and job enlargement. At least one company finds it useful to record the leaver's number of accidents and another records the number of suggestions made and accepted.

Leavers can also be classified according to training, earnings (including overtime and bonuses), type of work and skill category.

By department

For analytical puposes, each department should be considered as a totally independent entity. The question in analysing the causes of labour turnover may then no longer be why people are leaving but why they are leaving a particular department. This discovery can transform the whole problem and give a clue for reducing it.

A more detailed departmental breakdown of the labour force according to length of service and separated by sex is of help, in that it shows the size of the hard core. The particular value of a periodic return of this nature is that it highlights those departments in which it is proving difficult to get labour to settle. The analysis of a department by age groups and grades within the department will provide information of value when assessing the adequacy of salary levels, the effects of clerical work improvement programmes or when considering manpower planning problems.

Turnover percentages, excluding transfers, for each department can be included on the labour strength returns (see Chapter 3) so that Personnel can keep constantly informed of turnover trends in each department. Some firms also record a three-month moving average so that Personnel can take this number and simply multiply it by four to get the annual turnover at any time. At the end of each year these figures are analysed further.

By travelling time

A check on specific labour turnover rates related to the travelling time involved for the former employee may indicate what limits should be made in taking on employees living some distance from the company.

Time

A record of the time of year people leave sometimes helps to determine the factors causing turnover and, incidentally, helps in planning recruitment. By drawing a graph of turnover, according to date, it is possible to identify peaks which can then be associated with some internal or external factor which may have been the cause.

Identifying leavers

Employers need to be concerned with more than the number of those who have left. The type of individuals who leave may be of much more significance. The quality of the employee, for example, should be indicated somehow to help determine whether or not key men are being lost while the mediocre remain. A few firms determine this by relating the employee's rate of pay with tenure.

Age is an important consideration, to determine whether or not the company is losing younger men on whom it is depending. Age may also distinguish any particular age group where turnover is high in comparison with national figures or with other figures in the district for that age group. The rate of wastage tends to decline as age increases. This may be connected with length of service, but there is some evidence that age is quite a separate factor.

Length of service is particularly important as labour turnover, in general, is highest in the early months of employment. If it is very high in the first few weeks one may expect that selection techniques are poor or induction inadequate. If turnover is high in the early months, poor training methods or too short a training period may be the cause. If, on the other hand, long-service employees are seen to be leaving, morale may be low. Perhaps promotional policies, salary structure, welfare facilities or working conditions may be the factors.

Survival indices

It is felt by many that the length of service is, in fact, the most important factor in voluntary leaving rates. That is to say, leaving rates are very high in the first few weeks or months of employment and decrease with length of service. This rule applies regardless of the employee's age; a man of fifty is as liable to leave in his third year of service as a man of twenty-five in the same circumstances.

For this reason it is useful to show the percentage of employees engaged in any one year who are still with the firm in succeeding years. The so-called 'half-life survival index' is used to measure the time that elapses before a batch of entrants is reduced by termination to half its original size. It thus emphasises survival time rather than numbers surviving and avoids some of the defects of using a percentage for comparison purposes between different organisations and different entrants. The quarter-life can be obtained from a distribution of leavers at the same time as the half-life with very little extra effort.

Assessing the Cost

The financial cost of labour turnover can be calculated in various ways, but whatever figure is arrived at invariably exceeds estimates and may be much more than is ever calculated. But a calculation of the cost is important, as it is necessary to determine whether it would be more economical to change company policy or correct the factors responsible for unrest. Having said that, however, it should be added that there are other very good reasons for stabilising the labour force. Constant turnover has a tendency to demoralise remaining employees who can – and do – exploit apparent shortages of experienced workers for high salaries. Customer servicing may suffer. Customers may be disturbed by frequent staff changes and sales be lost because the sales force is not stable.

An assessment of the costs involved in labour turnover must take into account most or all of the following factors:

1   The cost of recruitment, selection and engagement (this should include the actual cost of advertising, agency fees, application and reference forms, medical examination, travel expenses, and so on. Selection will include the cost of time spent in discussing the vacancy, reading applications and interviewing)
2   The cost of induction
3   The expense of training and supervising new employees
4   The low output of trainees
5   The cost of overtime worked as a result of staff shortage
6   The cost of lost output when replacements are not available
7   Increased wastage and spoilage
8   Higher rate of accidents among trainee operatives
9   Lowered morale because new employees do not immediately acquire and accept the company's traditions

It is a good idea to itemise the costs in various categories, such as recruitment, selection and engagement, induction, job training and termination for example, which can be further broken down into actual costs. Selection, for instance, could include advertising costs, agency fees, applications and reference forms, medical examinations, security or credit investigations, company identification badges, photographs, equipment (safety goggles, protective clothing, etc), travel expenses, and so on. It is also necessary to consider the time of senior managers involved in interviewing and the foreman's time in teaching and supervising a new man – time that could be spent much more productively.

One must also take into account other, less obvious, costs such as increased wastage and spoilage, idle machinery, uneven production, increase in maintenance and depreciation of equipment, higher rate of accidents among newcomers, lower output from both a man who is about to leave and from the inexperienced newcomer. While his contribution remains low, he does not fully recover his proportion of fixed overheads.

Figure 8:1 Termination of employment form

This is a four-copy set: one copy to the personnel department, one to the wages department, one to the timekeeper and one for filing (George Cohen 600 Group)

From _____

To (2) Personnel Department

Employee's full name	Company	Department
	Depot	Clock number

By employee

I give notice of my intention to leave your employment on _____

Countersigned _____ Date _____ Signed _____ Employee
For the company

By employer

This confirms _____ week's notice given to this employee to leave our service on _____

Signed _____ Date _____ Signed _____ Employee
For the company

Reason for termination of employment

Special instructions on payments of wages, etc, and for disposal of P45 and pay due

Figure 8:2   Notice of termination report

Reasons for leaving are printed on the back of the 'notice of termination of employment' section

Part 1   **TO WAGES DEPARTMENT**   Date _____

PRELIMINARY NOTICE OF LEAVING

Please note that the undermentioned employee will be leaving on the date indicated. P45 and any monies payable should NOT be handed over until clearance (Part 3) is received from the Personnel Department

Employee's name _____   Clock No /Staff No _____

Department _____   Date of leaving _____
                                 Time _____
                                 Signed _____

Part 2   **NOTICE OF TERMINATION OF EMPLOYMENT**

Employee's name _____   Department _____

Clock No /Staff No _____   Occupation _____

Staff No _____

Length of service _____   Date of leaving _____

                                 Time _____

Member of Pension Scheme ? _____   Pensions Department notified? _____

Reason for leaving _____

Code No _____

Work Report _____

Character Report _____

Would you recommend re-engagement _____

ALL COMPANY'S EQUIPMENT RETURNED IN GOOD ORDER _____

                Head of Department's signature _____

                Personnel Officer's signature _____

(N.B. ALL THE ABOVE **MUST** BE COMPLETED BEFORE THE EMPLOYEE CAN LEAVE)

Part 3   **TO WAGES DEPARTMENT**   Date _____

                      CLEARANCE

Please note that the undermentioned employee is now authorised to collect pay and P45

Name _____   Clock No /Staff No _____

Date of leaving _____ Time _____ Signed _____

Holiday money due _____   Personnel Officer

TO BE RETURNED TO THE PERSONNEL DEPARTMENT

Figure 8:2 *continued*

REASONS FOR LEAVING

A   DISCHARGE

    1 Unsuitable

    2 Disciplinary reasons

    3 Redundancy

          (a) Shortage of materials

          (b) Seasonal fluctuations

          (c) Recession of trade

          (d) Other reasons

B   RESIGNATION

    4 Remuneration

    5 Hours of work

    6 Physical conditions of working (e.g. lighting, temperature, di t posture)

    7 Dissatisfaction with job

    8 Relationship with –

          (a) Fellow-workers

          (b) Supervisors

    9 Personal betterment

   10 Transport difficulties

   11 Housing difficulties

   12 Domestic responsibilities

   13 Illness or accident

   14 Marriage

   15 Pregnancy

   16 Moving from district

   17 Retirement

   18 Death

   19 Cause unknown

When there is more than one reason for leaving,
the dominant reason should be recorded

Figure 8:3   Composite form for resignations/retirements/dismissals/death
Including clearance for leave, car loans, season ticket loan etc. (Greater London Council)

GREATER LONDON COUNCIL
Department of Public Health Engineering

RESIGNATIONS/RETIREMENTS/DISMISSAL/DEATH – FACE SHEET

Name _____ Grade _____

L.D.S. _____ LOC/DIV. _____

		Date		Remarks
a)	Notice period			
b)	Senior Officers aware			
c)	Replacement			
d)	Acknowledgement letter/ valadictory letter/enclosures			
e)	Committee report			
f)	P280			
g)	Annual leave, etc. (CSF.14)			
h)	Leaver's book			
i)	Contact Officer for:			
	(i) Home address			
	(ii) Leave Card			
	(iii) Local Government?			
	(iv) Return of I.D. Cards			
j)	Car Loan?			
k)	Season Ticket Loan?			
l)	TR/SUP/109 to TR			
m)	Action on last day:			
	(i) Remove index/overtime/ sickness cards			
	(ii) Remove from S/list			
	(iii) Remove from salary list			
	(iv) Delete from probationary list			
n)	Final cheque + P45			

Figure 8:4   Certificate P45, particulars of employee leaving
Part 1 of this Inland Revenue form is sent to the tax office immediately upon termination of employment. See also Figure 3:3

INCOME TAX
PARTICULARS OF EMPLOYEE LEAVING

PART 1

1. Employer's PAYE reference	District number	Reference number

2. Employee's National Insurance number
(copy from Deduction Card)

3. Employee's surname   *(Enter in BLOCK letters)*   Mr. Mrs. Miss etc.

Employee's first two forenames   *(Enter in BLOCK letters)*

4. Date of leaving *(Enter in figures)*	Day	Month	Year 19

5. Code at date of leaving If on Week 1 (Month 1) basis also enter "X" in box marked "Wk. 1 (or Month 1)"	Code	Wk. 1 (or Month 1)

6. Last entries on Deduction Card *If Week 1 (Month 1) basis applies complete item 7 instead*	Week or Month No.	Week	Month
	Total pay to date	£	p
	Total tax to date	£	p

7. Week 1 (Month 1) basis applies	Total pay in this employment	£	p
	Total tax deducted in this employment	£	p

8. Works Number	9. Branch, Department, Contract, etc.

10. Employee's private address

11. I certify that the particulars entered at items 1 to 9 above are correct.

Employer

Address

Date

INSTRUCTIONS TO EMPLOYER
1. Complete this form (including the shaded boxes) if a code (other than NI) is in use when an employee leaves. Take care that the carbon entries on Parts 2 and 3 are legible.
2. Enter the code (number and letter) at item 5.
3. If the employee was engaged after 6 April last include in item 6 the pay and tax notified to you in respect of previous employments.
4. **Detach PART 1 and send it to your Tax Office IMMEDIATELY.**
5. **Hand PARTS 2 AND 3 (unseparated) to the employee WHEN HE LEAVES.**
6. If the employee has died, please enter "D" in this box ▶ and send **ALL THREE PARTS** of this form (unseparated) immediately to your Tax Office.

P45   HPB 1166 7/77

For Tax District use

For Centre use		
Amended	M/E	P

Figure 8:5   Employer's form for calculation of redundancy payment and worker's receipt (Department of Employment form RP3)

Department of Employment
Employment Protection (Consolidation) Act 1978

EMPLOYER'S CALCULATION OF REDUNDANCY PAYMENT AND EMPLOYEE'S RECEIPT

NOTES   *1*   *If redundancy payment is being reduced because of pension DO NOT USE THIS FORM. Please ask the office which issued this form for the pensions form RP 3(Pen).*
   2   *The calculation of payments not arising under the Redundancy Payments Act should be excluded from this form.*

Name of employer   ....
   ....
   ....

Employee's surname   ....   initials   ....

Employee's address   ....

Employee's date of birth   ....

Employee's employment began on   ....   and terminated during the week ending Saturday   ....   19......
Non-reckonable periods (employment abroad, on strike, service with the Armed Forces—see guidance in the booklet "*The Redundancy Payments Scheme*")

from..   to   ....   reason   ....

PART I — CALCULATION OF REDUNDANCY PAYMENT
   (See guidance in the booklet "*The Redundancy Payments Scheme*")

1   Total reckonable employment (exclude employment before age 18. *If more than 20 years' employment,*
   enter "20")   ....   years

2   Number of weeks' pay due   ....   weeks

3   Amount of a week's pay (*see booklet*)
   (1)   before applying £110 limit   £....................
   (2)   after applying £110 limit   £....................

4   Amount of redundancy payment (item 2 × item 3(2))   £....................
   NOTE:-   If the employee was aged at least 64 years and one month (man)/59 years and one month (woman) on the Saturday in the week in which the employment terminated, items 5, 6 and 7 below should be completed.

5   Number of complete months by which employee's age exceeds 64 (man)/59 (woman)
   on the Saturday in the week in which the employment terminated   ....months

6   Amount by which redundancy payment is to be reduced $\frac{(\text{item 4} \times \text{item 5})}{12}$ £....................

7   Adjusted amount of redundancy payment (item 4 minus item 6)   £....................

PART II — EMPLOYEE'S RECEIPT FOR REDUNDANCY PAYMENT

Warning—Do not sign this receipt until you have actually received the full amount stated or you may be penalised.

I acknowledge that the redundancy payment amounting to £....................................

was made to me on (date)....................................   Signature   ....

                                                                    Date..

NOTE: If more than one copy of this form is prepared for payment, the top copy receipted by the employee should accompany the claim for rebate on form RP2

RP 3   TS&Co.Ltd. 52-0-0 2/78

Figure 8:6   Claim Form for Rebate from the Redundancy Fund
(Department of Employment form RP2)

DEPARTMENT OF EMPLOYMENT

CLAIM FOR REBATE FROM REDUNDANCY FUND

Employment Protection (Consolidation) Act 1978

When paying rebate please
quote reference number

| MLH No. |
| SIC Order No. |

Full title of firm *(in block capitals please)* ....

....

Address ....

Nature of business .... Telephone number ....

To:—

1   I certify that the employees whose names are listed overleaf (and on continuation sheets numbered .... to ....)

  (1) (a) have not been re-employed either with this firm, or with an associated employer, or with a new owner of this firm's business (or any separate identifiable part of its business), or

     (b) if they have been so re-employed, that they have not remained beyond the end of the trial period. (see Note 5); and

  (2) terminated on the dates shown in Column 6 in each case; and

  (3) were entitled to redundancy payments in accordance with the Employment Protection (Consolidation) Act 1978 and

  (4) received those payments on the dates shown in the receipt portion of the enclosed statements (forms RP3/RP3(Pen)) which show how entitlement was calculated.

2   I have marked with an *, at the beginning of the relevant line on the reverse, the entry in respect of any employee who refused an offer of further employment, or ended (or gave notice to end) such employment during the trial period (see Notes 5 and 7 of the tear-off notes).   **Please tick box if this applied** ☐

3   I understand that to establish my rights to any rebate it may be necessary for you to refer to information given by me to the Inland Revenue and other Government departments and I hereby give my consent to the disclosure of such information for this purpose only.

4   Tax district office/computer centre .... Tax ref no. ....

5   I also certify that none of the redundancy payments to which this claim refers is awaiting a decision of an industrial tribunal.

6   I claim rebate amounting to £........................... (41% of the total of col 8 overleaf) and declare that no other claim has been made in respect of the service of these employees between the dates shown in columns 5 and 6.

Signature of employer ....

Position in firm (eg Director, Company Secretary etc) .... Date ....

FOR OFFICIAL USE

To the RFO ....RP2 and RP3/RP3(Pen) checked ....initials   Date ....

I certify that forms RP1, RP2 and RP3/RP3(Pen) have been checked and that any necessary amendments which have been made to the claim have been agreed with the employer. No previous claim has been received in respect of any of the employees listed overleaf (and on continuation sheets numbered .... to............................)

Claim is approved for payment £.. Approving Officer ....

Office ....   Date ....

FOR USE IN REGIONAL FINANCE OFFICE

Cashier please pay £... Dr ....

Authorising Officer .... Date ....

Paid by payable order number .... Dated ....

RP 2

Figure 8:6 *continued*

Claim for rebate from Redundancy Fund

IMPORTANT — MEN and WOMEN should be listed separately

Name and initials of employee (state whether Mr Mrs or Miss) 1	Occupation 2	National insurance number 3	Date of birth 4	Date employment began (See Note(a)) 5	Date of termination (See Note (b)) 6	Amount of week's pay (See Note(c)) 7	Redundancy payment 8	FOR OFFICIAL USE 9
1						£	£	
2								
3								
4								
5								
6								
7								
8								
9								
10								
11								
12								
13								
14								
15								
						TOTAL		

NOTES

(a) The date sought is the start of the period of continuous employment, to which the payment relates, with the dismissing employer, an associated employer or a previous owner of the business, except that no account should be taken of any service in respect of which a redundancy payment has already been made (see declaration at item 6 overleaf).

(b) If these entries are carbon copies of those in the form RP1 but the actual date of termination is different please write in the necessary amendment — See also note 6 on the tear-off.

(c) The amount of a week's pay should be calculated according to the rules set out in Appendix C of the booklet "The Redundancy Payments Scheme".

1852 2/78 GBR LTD

Figure 8:7   Notice of intention to claim rebate from the Redundancy Fund
(Department of Employment form RP1)

Department of Employment
Employment Protection (Consolidation) Act 1978

NOTICE OF INTENTION TO CLAIM REBATE FROM THE REDUNDANCY FUND
Full title of firm
(in block capitals) ....

Address ....

.... Telephone No. ....

To: ....
....

1   I declare that the employees whose names are listed overleaf (and on the continuation sheets numbered ....
to ....) are expected to be dismissed, as defined in Note 2 on the tear-off page retained by me, on the
dates shown in column 6 of each sheet. Each has been employed throughout the stated period for either —

Please tick the appropriate box

(1) a continuous period of two years as in Note 3(1) on the tear-off page, or

(2) a continuous period of five years as in Note 3(2) on the tear-off page

*Please tick if offers of further
work are likely*

2   I expect that some of the listed employees will be offered further work by this firm, an
associated employer, or a successor owner of the business (see Note 4 on tear-off page)

3   The reason for the anticipated dismissal (see Note 5 on tear-off page) has been ticked in the appropriate box
below:—

(1) Closure of the establishment

(2) Removal of the establishment to another area

(3) Reduction in labour force at the establishment due to

(a) general reduction in level of activities

(b) reduction in activities on which the employees engaged

(c) changes in methods of work eg mechanisation, automation

(d) elimination of slack in workloads

(4) Other reasons (specified at item 4 below)

4   Additional information (see Notes 5–6 on tear-off page).

5   Address at which the employees work if different from above ....
....

6   I understand that to establish my right to any rebate it may be necessary for you to refer to information given by
me to the Inland Revenue and other Government departments and I hereby give my consent to the disclosure of
such information for this purpose.

Tax district office/computer centre .... Tax ref No. ....

*7   The reason for the delay in submitting this notification is (see Note 1 on tear-off portion)

Signature of employer .... Date ....

Position in firm (eg director, company secretary) ....

* *Delete if inapplicable*

RP 1

Figure 8:7 *continued*

List of employees who are expected to become redundant and be entitled to statutory redundancy payments

IMPORTANT — MEN and WOMEN should be listed separately

Name and Initials of employee (state whether Mr Mrs or Miss) (See Note (a)) 1	Occupation 2	National insurance number 3	Date of birth 4	Date employment began (See Note (b)) 5	Date of termination 6	Amount of week's pay (See Note (c)) 7	FOR OFFICIAL USE 8
1						£	
2							
3							
4							
5							
6							
7							
8							
9							
10							
11							
12							
13							
14							
15							

NOTES

(a) Entries in columns 1 to 7 may be carbon copied to form RP2.

(b) The date sought is the start of the period of continuous employment, to which the payment relates, with the dismissing employer or an associated employer or a previous owner of the business.

(c) The amount of a week's pay should be calculated according to the rules explained in Appendix C of the booklet "The Redundancy Payments Scheme". If it is not possible at this stage to calculate the amount in any case, please leave the relevant col 7 space blank and forward the information as soon as possible. Please seek early advice through the office shown above item 1 overleaf, about calculations involving piece workers or shift or rota workers.

FOR OFFICIAL USE

	INITIALS	DATE
RP 1 received		
RP 5 sent		

	INITIALS	DATE
RP 2/3 received		
RP 2/3 to RFO		
RP 2/3 received		
RP 2/3 to RFO		
RP 2/3 received		
RP 2/3 to RFO		
RP 2/3 received		
RP 2/3 to RFO		
RP 2/3 received		
RP 2/3 to RFO		
RP 2/3 received		
RP 2/3 to RFO		

1852 2/78 GBR LTD

Figure 8:8   Written statement offering redundant workers other work
The offer must be made to the employee while he is still employed by the employer
and the date completed should indicate this

This statement sets out particulars of the terms and conditions on which (name of
employer) is offering (name of employee) employment to begin on——

Brief description of employment

Location

Scale or rate of remuneration (or the method of calculating remuneration)

Intervals at which remuneration is paid

Normal hours of work (and any other terms and conditions relating to hours of work)

Holidays and holiday pay

Terms and conditions relating to incapacity for work due to sickness or injury, and
sick pay

Pensions and pension schemes

Amount of notice of termination to be given by

   (*a*) Employee

   (*b*) Employer

Signed

Date

Figure 8:9   Personal Warning Form (Kalamazoo)

WRITTEN WARNING		
Employee's Name	No.	Department

This is to confirm the warning given to you on   in the presence of (Your

representative)   details of which are given below

You are advised that (any re-occurrence of such behaviour)/(if you do not show any significant improvement in

this matter in the next   months) the matter will be referred to   (Manager)
and will lead to further disciplinary action.

A copy of this letter will be placed on your personal file (but will be **discounted** if improvement is shown in the

time stated above.)

Details.

Signed _____ Position _____ Date _____

for _____

Copy of warning received _____ _____ (Employee or
                                                                                                        Representative)

Kalamazoo 2136-911

Figure 8:10   Personal record of warnings

The record illustrated here shows a space where warnings are recorded and the number of warnings given is signalled on the visible edge in red. Where a visible margin shows an excessively long red line – representing a considerable number of warnings – this fact is immediately seen and the need for some further disciplinary action is apparent (Kardex Systems (UK) Limited)

Date	Reason 1 2 3 4 5 6	Remarks	Year	Number of days worked	Total earnings	Average earnings per week
			19			
			19			
			19			
			19			
			19			
			19			
			19			
			19			
			19			
			19			
			19			
			19			
			19			
			19			
			19			
			19			

Record of warnings — Summary

Reason code: 1 Defective work   3 Lateness   5 Disobedience
2 Conduct   4 Absence   6 Carelessness

SX	Department	Name	Clock number	Ratings (lower) Number of warnings (upper)

Number of warnings (upper): 2 4 5 6 7 8 9 10 11 12 13 14 15 16 17 18 19 20

Ratings (lower): 0 | 10 | 20 | 30 | 40 | 50 | 60 | 70 | 80 | 90 | 100

Figure 8:11 Form MP1 – claim for rebate of maternity pay

	Redundancy Payments Office
	DEPARTMENT OF EMPLOYMENT REDUNDANCY PAYMENTS OFFICE 1 BARNSBURY ROAD LONDON, N1 0EX.

Department of Employment

EMPLOYMENT PROTECTION ACT 1975

CLAIM FOR REBATE OF MATERNITY PAY

Full name of firm ....

Address ....

....

Name, position and telephone no. of person to be contacted in case of query

....

A   Details of employee in respect of whom rebate is claimed

1   Name ....

2   Address ....

....

3   Nature and place of employment ....

....

4   National Insurance No. ....

5   Income Tax reference No. ....

6   *Date when current period of continuous employment began ....

7   Expected date of confinement ....
         (as notified to employer)

8   Date maternity pay period commenced ....

9   †If employment ceased before maternity pay period commenced:

a   give date on which it ceased ....

b   state reasons for employment ceasing

*An employee is continuously employed if she works under a contract of employment which normally involves employment for 16 hours or more weekly, or 8 hours or more if she has been with the same employer for 5 years or more. Employees who do not satisfy this requirement would not be entitled to maternity pay. For cases of doubt and difficult cases see booklet "Continuous Employment and the Week's Pay", available from Jobcentres, Employment Offices and Unemployment Benefit Offices.

†Under Section 35 (3) an employee who is dismissed before the 11th week before expected confinement is still entitled to maternity pay if the reason for dismissal is that she is not capable because of her condition of continuing to work, or she would be in breach of a statutory restriction by continuing to work, and if she would have had 2 years continuous employment at the 11th week had she not been dismissed.

Form MP1   (06288)

Figure 8:11 *continued*

B   Calculation of Maternity Pay

NOTE: If maternity pay has been paid following an award of an Industrial Tribunal paragraphs 1 and 6 to 8 only should be
          completed

1   *Gross amount of normal week's pay £ ....

2   Deduct:

      1/10th of week's pay   £..

      †Flat rate national insurance
        maternity allowance   £..

      Total   £..

3   Gross weekly amount of Maternity Pay payable by employer (1–2)   £..

4   Number of weeks for which payment made (maximum 6)   ....

5   Total gross amount of Maternity Pay payable by employer   £..
      (item 3 x item 4)

6   Amount awarded by industrial tribunal (if appropriate)   £..

      – please attach copy of award if available (this will be returned)
        or state reference no. of case and date and place of hearing

      ....

7   Employee deductions (totals for whole of pay period or amount of tribunal award)

      NI contributions   £..

      Income Tax   £..

      Any other agreed deductions
      (specify)   £..

      Total   £..

8   **Total net amount due to employee** (item 5 or item 6 – item 7)   £..

9   Date on which payment or, if paid in instalments, final payment of maternity pay was made

      ....

*For difficult cases see booklet "Continuous Employment and 'a Week's Pay' ", available from Jobcentres, Employment Offices
and Unemployment Benefit Offices.

†This amount is deducted whether it is due to the employee or not.   The amount is currently £14.70 per week but this is liable
to change and should be checked with your local Social Security Office.   No deduction should be made in respect of earnings
related supplements.

NOTE: Claims for rebate should not be submitted until the full payment period is complete (item 4) and the employee has
          received the full amount due (item 8)

(06288)

Figure 8:11 *continued*

C   **Calculation of Amount of Rebate Claimed**

1   Total gross amount paid by employer £..
(amount at item B5 or amount of
tribunal award, as appropriate)

2   Total secondary (employers) national £..
insurance contributions paid by
employer on amount at C1

3   Amount claimed as rebate (1 + 2)   £..

D   **Claim**

The above named employee was absent during the period of the claim (item B4).   She appears to be entitled to maternity

pay in accordance with the Employment Protection Act 1975 and I have paid to her the sum of £ ....

being the gross amount shown at item C1 above less the deductions specified at B7* which I have paid over to the

appropriate authorities.   Receipt(s) for this payment is/are attached.   No previous claim has been made for the same weeks

for the same person.

I claim rebate of £ .... being the amount calculated at C3 above.

Signed .... Date..

Position in firm ....
(eg Director, Secretary, Personnel Manager)

*Industrial tribunal awards are subject to deductions for income tax and National Insurance contributions.

This form is to be sent to:
(Address of Local Redundancy Payments Office)

DEPARTMENT OF EMPLOYMENT
REDUNDANCY PAYMENTS OFFICE
1 BARNSBURY ROAD
LONDON, N1 0EX.

NOT LATER THAN 6 MONTHS AFTER DATE AT B9.

(06288)

Figure 8:12   Employee's Receipt for Maternity Pay
(Department of Employment Form MP1(R))

DEPARTMENT OF EMPLOYMENT

EMPLOYEE'S RECEIPT FOR MATERNITY PAY

Name and address of Employee ....

....

....

Name and address of Employer ....

....

....

I acknowledge that maternity pay amounting to £ ....

(net after deductions of income tax £ .... and NI contributions £ ....

for the period   /   /   to   /   /   was paid to me on   /   /   *

Signature ....

Date ....

*If payment was made in instalments give date of final payment. Do not sign this
form until you have received your full entitlement of pay.

NOTE: Evidence of receipt of payment is required. If it is not possible to
obtain a receipt in this form please contact the office indicated below
for advice.

Local Redundancy Payments Office

DEPARTMENT OF EMPLOYMENT
REDUNDANCY PAYMENTS OFFICE
1 BARNSBURY ROAD
LONDON, N1 0EX.

MP I (R)   Bas 33981/1/527458 270m 3/77 CI

Figure 8:13 Termination interview form

Part *A* comprises a standard classification of reasons for leaving and a coupon to send to the personnel department. Statistics are collected and an intelligent use of them has played a major part in reducing the cost of labour turnover. The form is completed by the division or department concerned and is sent with the staff advice arising from the termination of employment to the personnel department

TERMINATION INTERVIEW REPORT	
A To be completed by the employing department	
Name	Department
Date of birth	Section
Date of engagement	Present job title
Job title on joining	Present salary
Latest date available for interview	Present salary group
Effectiveness in present position	Graduate/nongraduate
Promotability/potential for advancement	MPT/support
Termination interview – Highly desirable/useful	

B To be completed by employee relations department		
Leaver's impression of the company Including training, salary progression, job experience, career development		
Reasons for leaving		
Relationship with manager		
Relationship with colleagues		
New company	Job title	Salary
Signed	Employee relations department	Date
Manager's comments (if any)		
Signed		Date

Figure 8:14   Analysis of labour turnover
This is one of several forms recommended by the British Institute of Management for analysing labour turnover by reason, length of service and sex

MONTHLY ANALYSIS

Month of ....19..........

	CUMULATIVE LENGTH OF SERVIC									
	less than 1 month M* F*		1–3 months M F		4–12 months M F		1–2 years M F		2–5 years M F	

DISCHARGED EMPLOYEES
  1 **Unsuitable**
  2 **Disciplinary reasons**
  3 **Redundant**										

RESIGNATION
(**Uncontrollable**)
 	
  4 **Changes in personal circumstances**
  Domestic/marriage/pregnancy
  Illness/accident
  Death/retirement
  Move from district
  Transport/housing difficulties										

RESIGNATION
(**Controllable**)
 	
  5 **Job dissatisfaction**
  Remuneration and/or pension scheme
  Nature of work
  Lack of prospects
  Hours of work
  Physical working conditions (e.g. lighting, temperature, dirt, posture)
  Relationship with supervisors and fellow-workers										

RESIGNATION 6 **Other reasons**										
TOTALS										

•M=MALE
•F=FEMALE

Figure 8:14 *continued*

OF LEAVERS

E				
	over 5 years		Total	
	M	F	M	F

1 FORMULAE

$$\text{Monthly Labour Turnover percentage (Employee wastage)} = \frac{\text{No. of leavers during month}}{\text{average no. employed during month}} \times 100$$

$$\text{Monthly Labour Turnover expressed as an annual rate} = \text{Monthly Labour Turnover percentage} \times 12$$

2 LABOUR TURNOVER CALCULATIONS

Monthly Labour Turnover Rate MALE: % FEMALE: %	
Annual Labour Turnover Rate MALE: % FEMALE: %	
Total no. of leavers previous month	= M F
Total no. of new engagements during month	= M F
Total employed at beginning of month	= M F
Total employed at end of month	= M F
Average no. employed during month	= M F

3 NOTES

Temporary workers engaged for specific tasks of less than 1 month's duration should be <u>excluded</u>

Seasonal workers should be <u>included</u>

Part-time workers regularly employed for less than 30 hours per week should be included, but each such employee reckoned as <u>one half</u>

9

Maintaining the System

Any new system must be understood and accepted, not only by the people responsible for its successful day-to-day operation but also by others, not directly concerned with Personnel, whose activities require the use of personnel records. It is essential that all staff are educated to the need for new procedures so that they understand what is being attempted and appreciate the results to be achieved. This is particularly true when computerised systems are being introduced. Even people who are anxious to cooperate may simply not understand why existing procedures must be changed to what may appear to be unnecessarily complicated ones. They may have difficulty in consolidating their existing records, if any; they may neglect to provide complete information; they may make unreasonable assumptions.

Policy Statements

It is most important to develop a policy to ensure that all plans, policies, standards, programmes and procedures concerned with personnel are complied with by line and functional managers, and that corrective action is taken where necessary.

A policy statement must go beyond stating general aspirations. It should make clear to management, in all areas and at all levels, the company's intention and how it is expected to be carried out. It is *not* as it appears to be in many companies, a list of the personnel department's functions.

A comprehensive personnel policy statement would cover the following:

Company organisation
Management structure
Recruitment
Selection
Promotion

Accident prevention (including liability and notification)
Provision of tools, equipment and protective clothing
Training

Transfers
Holidays
Remuneration
Wage increases
Hours of work
Travel arrangements
Company vehicles
Complaints procedures
Loans
Discipline (drinking, gambling, etc)
Absenteeism and lateness

Further education
Management development
Merit rating
Performance appraisal
Absenteeism
Parking
Physical examinations
Tests
Expenses and allowances
Period of notice
Dismissals
Redundancy
Retirement

Procedures Manuals

In addition to policy statements, a procedures manual should be made available to all those involved in completing and keeping personnel records, explaining how the records are grouped, what systems are used for indexing and filing each group, their location, the coding structure, the proper procedures for recording data, the procedures for transferring active files to semi-active and storage, and the period of retention. It should also contain an up-to-date list of all individuals in any way involved in the records, and should make clear what their responsibilities are.

The manuals should also show the origin of data for each report, the reporting path of information, report formats, users of each report, decisions for which information is necessary and copies of any special forms required to collect or report data.

Procedural changes always present problems and it is advisable to keep the procedures manual as a loose-leaf binder with typewritten pages which can be detached and replaced as needed.

Training

The subject of personnel records and forms should be given an important part in induction courses for both staff and management.

If newly introduced procedures tend to be more complicated than the existing system, in the introduction of computerised systems, for example, some additional training may be required to ensure that the employees understand the purpose of the change and the new procedures being introduced. A large number of people may be naturally against computerisation – because they do not understand what is being attempted, or they have seen poor results previously or it may create more clerical work on their part – or they may simply not accept the need for any change in existing methods.

Standard Letters

Standard letters can often serve the purpose of a form and help to reduce the clerical workload. It is important, however, that letters from Personnel do not appear impersonal. A standard format can be established which can be amended to suit particular circumstances.

Such letters can be used for routine activities, such as confirming letters of resignation, acknowledging applications for a vacancy, inviting candidates to an interview, and seeking references. Successful candidates are often informed personally or by telephone, but it is still advisable to confirm appointments with a letter. It is a normal courtesy, as soon as the vacancy is filled, to send a letter to all those who attended interviews informing them that their application was unsuccessful.

Letters inviting applicants to an interview should include instructions on where to report, including the gate number if there is more than one, and directions on how to reach the firm by public transport. Some firms include a pre-paid postcard for the applicant to return, indicating whether or not he will be able to attend the interview as arranged. If reimbursement of expenses involved is to be made, this should be stated in the letter. The receptionist can reimburse the applicant while he is waiting to be interviewed or before he leaves.

It is useful, incidentally, to have some literature about the company and working conditions as well as the current issue of the employee's journal in the waiting room. This may save a lot of needless questions at the interview.

Letters of appreciation and congratulations are very much appreciated by employees. It is pleasant to receive a personal letter on the occasion of a promotion, retirement or resignation, or before joining the firm. It is important, however, that such letters are personal and sincere.

Effectiveness of the System

The effectiveness of the personnel department should be continually assessed to help guide the actual work of personnel administration. The efficiency of the personnel procedure should not be difficult with accurate and accessible records. The value of a record of the interviewer's assessment of a new employee, for example, is in the comparison which can be made with subsequent performance. In this way a check is made on the success of selection procedures and interviews.

In the same way, the day-to-day working methods within the personnel department must be subject to the same tests of efficiency and productivity.

One should begin by looking at what is being done– and what is *not* being done – how it is done and why it is done in the way it is. Circumstances change all the time and it often happens that working arrangements continue to be followed even though they may have become unsuitable or unnecessary.

Are the people doing the right sort of jobs?
Are they using the best methods?
Are they always working under pressure?
Are some people always finding it necessary to stay after hours?

It is advisable to study the full utilisation of the office equipment. Is the office equipment used the right kind for the job? Is the office layout satisfactory? Is it possible to reduce the amount of ineffective time spent in walking or looking for information?

Confidential Records

Personnel records are considered confidential and should be treated as such by the personnel department staff. Their circulation should be strictly controlled. Any record withdrawn should be replaced by a temporary card indicating who has borrowed it, the date and, possibly, the purpose. For the same reason, staff dealing with personnel and wage records, including computer operators, are carefully selected and instructed properly to safeguard the interests of individual employees.

There should also be a quiet space for employees to discuss their personal affairs in private. Personnel staff should be approachable. They must be able to listen sympathetically to all kinds of queries, the weirdest interpretation of the rules and the 'special cases' that arise, and advise employees with special problems, no matter how petty these may sometimes be.

Under no circumstances should an employee be called from his work to report to the personnel office without some explanation of the reason. It is for personnel officers to get out of their offices occasionally to visit employees at their work.

It is relevant to mention here the need for courtesy and tact in dealing with employees in the personnel office, and this holds true for secretaries and clerks. Many people visiting the personnel department are nervous, particularly those applying for work or with personal problems. This is a fact that is too often forgotten by personnel office staff, even by those with long experience in personnel work.

Retention of Records

Just how long personnel records should be retained is a moot point. One needs to consider such factors as space, frequency with which the records are referred to, legal obligations, the particular circumstances of the company, the nature of the work and the firm's own restrictions on former employees – on working for competitors, for example.

Records of names of employees and dates of engagement should be kept permanently as should records of accidents and illnesses contracted as a direct result of working. Application forms of unsuccessful candidates (together with the reason for refusal) may be usefully kept for a short time (*a*) to be useful should a similar vacancy arise (*b*) to serve as back up material should the company face a claim for discrimination. Certain records concerning wages, working time and holidays should be kept for a period of at least three years. In normal circumstances, an employer would be quite justified in destroying any other personal records.

It is useful to establish a retention schedule for each record and to indicate where they are stored. The date for destroying each form can be printed on the form itself in small type.

Some firms identify their records as vital, important, useful or non-essential, and list their records in each category to determine the type of filing cabinets required for protection. Records can also be filed according to the time when they can be destroyed and a schedule prepared to advise Personnel when they no longer need to be kept. Incidentally, there is no reason why personnel records cannot be stored with those of other departments to save on storage costs.

The feasibility of microfilming records for the purpose of storage should also be considered. By reducing the size of documents by photography a company can save on storage space and considerable time can be saved if frequent reference is made to the material. On the other hand, it is difficult with microfilm to identify different coloured cards and impossible to add documents in their normal filing sequence after filming.

Microfilming is expensive, but so is storage space – a careful cost analysis should be undertaken. A quick estimate of saving may be made by comparing the cost with the value of the space taken up for storage multiplied by the number of years for which the records are kept. The cost of microfilming is determined by the volume or records – the number of sheets or cards to be microfilmed – plus the cost of preparing the records, the cost of inspection and retakes, the cost of replacing records in the files, transportation and packaging. It is also necessary to consider the cost of reading equipment or the use of a microfilm service bureau. The total cost should then be divided by the cubic feet of space and multiplied by years of retention.

Appendix 1

Publications

Her Majesty's Stationery Office and other non-profit making organisations publish a number of free and inexpensive booklets dealing with personnel administration. Listed here are some which may be of use to those in personnel departments who are concerned with records and forms.

Records and forms

HMSO, Health and Safety Executive – forms and publications. *Catalogue of Forms and Other Publications for use in Premises under the Factories Act 1961, Offices, Shops and Railway Premises Act 1963, and Related Legislation* (Sectional List No. 18) (London, HMSO). Free of charge.
British Institute of Management, *Records Retention* (London, BIM). Examines record retention, storage and disposal policies. Free of charge but available to collective subscribers only.
BACIE, *A guide to the Writing of Business Letters* (London, British Association for Commercial and Industrial Education)
Report Writing (London, BACIE)
Perry, P.J.C., *Hours into Minutes* (London, BACIE). A guide to committee documentation, including agendas, minutes and supplementary papers.
Ream, B., *A Guide to Employment Practices* (London, The Industrial Society)

Employment

Dyer, Barbara, *Producing an Employees' Handbook* (London, The Industrial Society)
Factories Act 1961. A short guide (London, HMSO)
The Industrial Society, *Legal Problems of Employment* (London, The Industrial Society)

Equal Opportunities Commission, *Guidance on Employment Advertising Practice* (Manchester, Equal Opportunities Commission)

Equal Opportunity Policies and Practices in Employment (Manchester, Equal Opportunities Commission)

Gough, J.S., *Interviewing in Twenty-six Steps* (London, BACIE). Includes useful checklist

HMSO, *Government Publications, Department of Employment* (Sectional List No. 21) (London HMSO). Free of Charge

Wage Administration

Board of Inland Revenue, *Employer's Guide to Pay as You Earn*. Free of charge.

Department of Health & Social Security, *Employer's Guide to Graduated National Insurance Contributions* (Leaflet NI 116). Free of charge

Boydell, T.H., *A Guide to Job Analysis* (London, BACIE)

National Board for Prices and Incomes, *Job Evaluation* (Report Number 83, Cmnd 3772) (London, HMSO 1968). Outlines the various work study techniques available and the degree of success in application

The Industrial Society, *Job Evaluation* (London, The Industrial Society)

Thomason, G.F., *Personnel Manager's Guide to Job Evaluation* (London, Institute of Personnel Management)

Pomeroy, J., *Sick Pay Schemes* (London, IPM)

Clark, F. Le Gros and Faubert, Carole, *Fringe Benefits for Pensioners* (London, IPM)

Innes, Irene, *Salary Management* (London, The Industrial Society)

HMSO, *Government Publications. Board of Inland Revenue* (Sectional List No. 29) (London, HMSO). Free of charge

Training

Jones, Sheila, *Design of Instruction* (London, HMSO)

Warr, P.B. and Bird, M.W., *Identifying Supervisory Training Needs* (London, HMSO)

Central Training Council, *Supervisory Training – A New Approach for Management* (A study by the Industrial Training Service) (London, HMSO)

Central Training Council, *An Approach to the Training and Development of Managers* (London, HMSO)

Central Training Council, *Training and Development of Managers* (London, HMSO)

Manpower Services Commission, *Training of Trainers* (London, Manpower Services Commission)

Manpower Planning

Gray, Daniel H., *Manpower Planning: An Approach to the Problem* (London, IPM)
Institute of Personnel Management, *Perspective in Manpower Planning* (London, IPM)
Department of Employment, *Company Manpower Planning* (Manpower Paper 1) (London, HMSO)

Computers

Mumford, Enid, *Living with a Computer* (London, IPM)
Mumford, Enid, *Computers, Planning and Personnel Management* (London, IPM)
Springall, Joan, *Personnel Records and the Computer* (London, IPM)
Wille, Edgar, *The Computer in Personnel Work* (London, IPM)

Statistics

Holman, Leonard J., *Basic Statistics for Personnel Managers* (London, IPM)
Reichmann, W.J., *Use and Abuse of Statistics* (Harmondsworth, Penguin)
Royal Society for the Prevention of Accidents, *Works Accident Statistics Records and Analysis (Part 2)* (Birmingham, ROSPA)

Safety

HMSO *Is my office safe?* (London, HMSO)
Royal Society for the Prevention of Accidents, *Safety at Work* (Birmingham, ROSPA)
Royal Society for the Prevention of Accidents, *Accident Record Cards* (Birmingham, ROSPA)

Appendix 2

Legislation affecting Employment

The texts of all legislation are available from HMSO

Welfare

Law Reform (Personal Injuries) Act 1948
Shops Acts 1950–1965
Factories Act 1961
Offices, Shops and Railway Premises Act 1963
Employer's Liability (Defective Equipment) Act 1969
Employer's Liability (Compulsory Insurance) Act 1969
Employment Medical Advisory Service Act 1972
Health and Safety at Work etc. Act 1974
Safety Representatives and Safety Committee Regulations 1977

Employment

Disabled Persons (Employment) Acts 1944 and 1958
Race Relations Acts 1965, 1968 and 1976
Redundancy Payments Act 1965
Employment and Training Act 1973
Rehabilitation of Offenders Act 1974
Trade Union & Labour Relations Act 1974 and 1976
Sex Discrimination Act 1975
Employment Protection Act 1975
Employment Protection (Consolidation) Act 1978

Wages

Truck Acts 1831, 1896 and 1940
Truck Amendment Act 1887
Fair Wages Resolutions 1891–1946
Shop Clubs Act 1902
Cheques Act 1957
Maintenance Orders Act 1958
Payment of Wages Act 1960
Equal Pay Act 1970 and 1975
Attachment of Earnings Act 1971

National Insurance

National Insurance Acts 1965, 1966, 1967, 1969, 1970, 1971, 1972
National Insurance (Industrial Injuries) Act 1965
National Insurance (Industrial Injuries) (Amendment) Act 1967
Ministry of Social Security Act 1966
Social Security Pensions Act 1975

Appendix 3

Useful Addresses

Advisory Conciliation and Arbitration Service (ACAS)

Head Office

Cleland House, Page Street, London SW1P 4ND
Tel: 01–211 3000

Northern Region

Westgate House, Westgate Road, Newcastle-upon-Tyne NE1 1TJ
Tel: 0632 612191

Cumbria	Tyne and Wear	Cleveland
Northumberland	Durham	

Yorkshire and Humberside Region

City House, Leeds LS1 4JH
Tel: 0532 38232

North Yorkshire	South Yorkshire
West Yorkshire	Humberside

South Eastern Region

Clifton House, 83–117 Euston Road, London NW1 2RB
Tel: 01–388 5100

Cambridgeshire	Hertfordshire	Hampshire
Norfolk	Essex	(except Ringwood)
Suffolk	Isle of Ely	Isle of Wight

Oxfordshire	Surrey	East Sussex
Buckinghamshire	Berkshire	West Sussex
Bedfordshire	Kent	

London Region

Clifton House, 83–117 Euston Road, London NW1 2RB
Tel: 01–388 5100
Greater London

South Western Region

16 Park Place, Clifton, Bristol BS8 1JP
Tel: 0272 211921

Gloucestershire	Cornwall	Dorset
Avon	Devon	Ringwood
Wiltshire	Somerset	

Midlands Region

Alpha Tower, Suffolk Street, Queensway, Birmingham B1 1TZ
Tel: 021–643 9911

Derbyshire (except	Leicester	Herefordshire and
High Peak District)	Northamptonshire	Worcestershire
Nottingham	Shropshire	West Midlands
Lincolnshire	Staffordshire	Metropolitan County
		Warwickshire

North Western Region

Boulton House, 17–21 Chorlton Street, Manchester M1 3HY
Tel: 061–228 3222

| Lancashire | Greater Manchester | High Peak District |
| Merseyside | Cheshire | of Derbyshire |

Scotland

Franborough House, 123–157 Bothwell Street, Glasgow G2 7JR
Tel: 041–204 2677

Wales

Phase 1, Ty Glas Road, Llanishen, Cardiff CF4 5PH
Tel: 0222 762636

Other

British Association for Commercial and Industrial Education
16 Park Crescent
London W1N 4AP

British Institute of Management
Management House
Parker Street
London WC2B 5PT

Commission for Racial Equality
Elliott House
10–12 Allington Street
London SW1E 5EH

Department of Employment
8 St James's Square
London SW1Y 4JB

Equal Opportunities Commission
Overseas House
Quay Street
Manchester M3 3HN

Health and Safety Commission
Baynards House
Chepstow Place
London W2

Her Majesty's Stationery Office
49 High Holborn
London WC1V 6HB

The Industrial Society
PO Box 1BQ
48 Bryanston Square
London W1H 1BQ

Institute of Personnel Management
Central House
Upper Woburn Place
London WC1 0HX

Institute of Training and Development
5 Baring Road
Beaconsfield
Bucks HP9 2NX

Royal Society for the Prevention of Accidents
Cannon House
The Priory
Queensway
Birmingham   B4 6BS

Index